MW00588371

Eight Lectures on Experimental Music

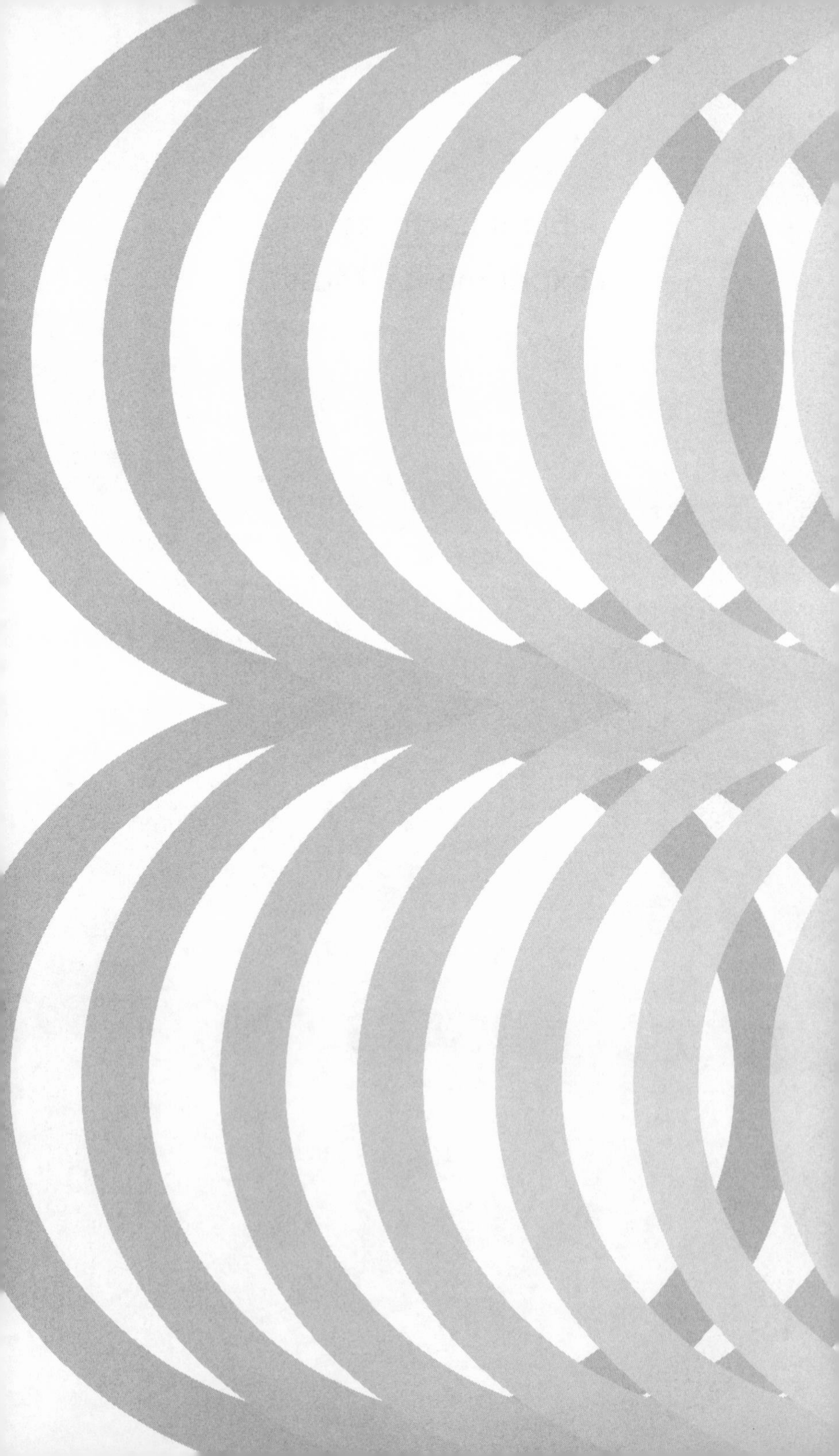

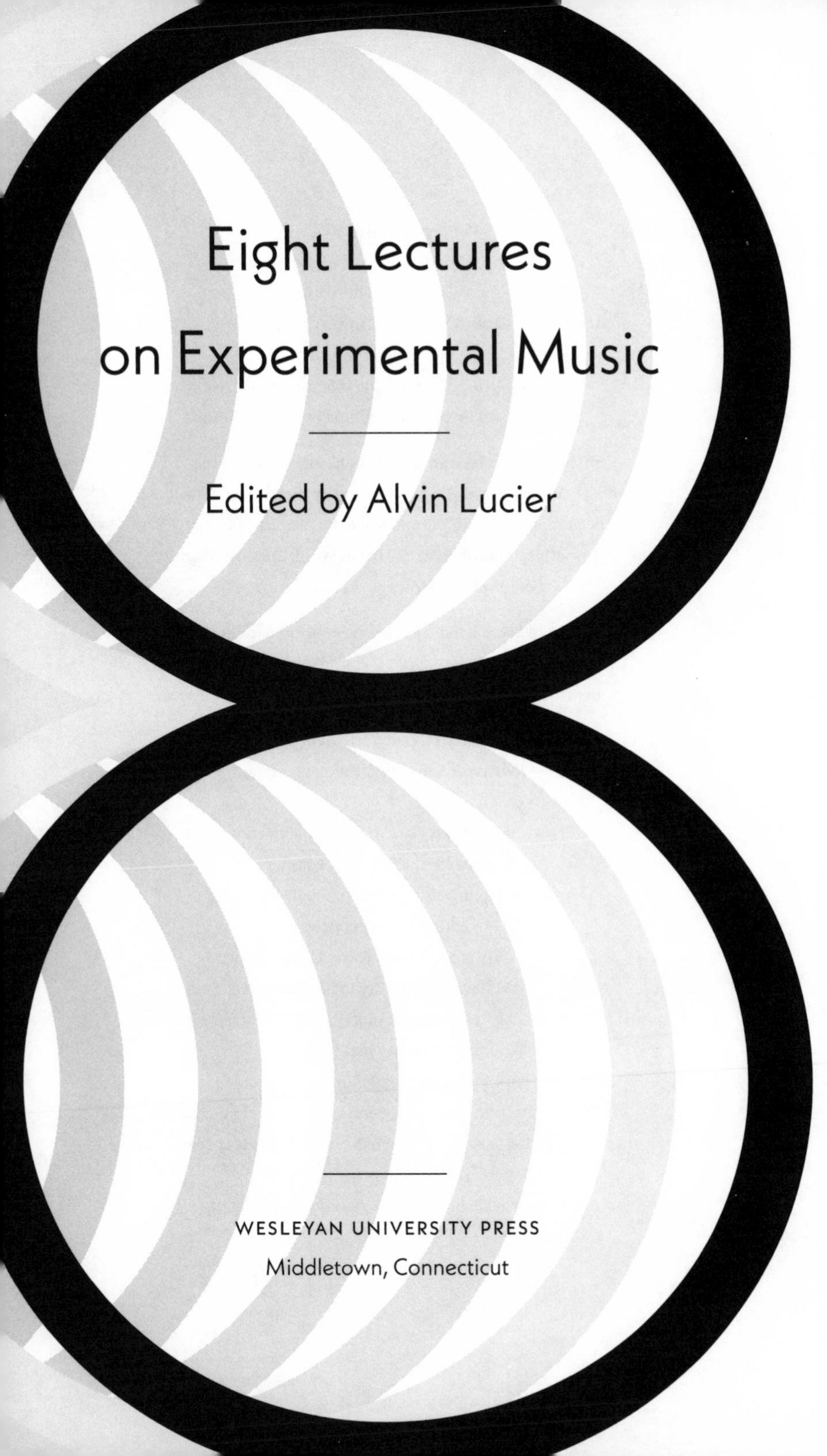

Eight Lectures on Experimental Music

Edited by Alvin Lucier

WESLEYAN UNIVERSITY PRESS
Middletown, Connecticut

Wesleyan University Press
Middletown CT 06459
www.wesleyan.edu/wespress

Manufactured in the United States of America
Designed and typeset in Calluna by Eric M. Brooks

Christian Wolff's lecture is to be published in his forthcoming book, *Occasional Pieces* (Oxford University Press, 2017). The lecture has been reprinted with permission from Oxford University Press. It was also published in Christian Wolff, *Cues: Writings & Conversations* (Cologne: MusikTexte, 1998).

Parts of Steve Reich's lecture were printed in his book *Writings on Music, 1965–2000* (Oxford University Press, 2002). Reprinted with permission from Oxford University Press.

Part of Steve Reich's lecture originally appeared in the *Kurt Weill Newsletter* (Fall 1992): 10 (2).

Library of Congress Cataloging-in-Publication Data
NAMES: Lucier, Alvin editor.
TITLE: Eight lectures on experimental music / edited by Alvin Lucier.
DESCRIPTION: Middletown, Connecticut: Wesleyan University Press, [2017] |
IDENTIFIERS: LCCN 2017019112 (print) | LCCN 2017021187 (ebook) | ISBN 9780819577641 (ebook) | ISBN 9780819577634 (cloth: alk. paper)
SUBJECTS: LCSH: Music—20th century—History and criticism.
CLASSIFICATION: LCC ML197 (ebook) | LCC ML197 .E33 2017 (print) | DDC 780.9/04—dc23
LC record available at https://lccn.loc.gov/2017019112

5 4 3 2 1

To

RICHARD K. WINSLOW,

who, with the calm of a deep sea diver,

changed the teaching of music at

Wesleyan and in the world

Contents

Introduction

One of the benefits of being the John Spencer Camp Professor of Music at Wesleyan is that each year you have a discretionary fund that you may use to enrich programs of your choice within the Music Department. Between 1989 and 2002, I invited eight composers whose music I featured in my lecture course, Music 109, Introduction to Experimental Music, to come to campus to talk about their work. The lectures were presented in the World Music Hall in the Center for the Arts at Wesleyan. Each was recorded and transcribed by a Music Department graduate student, then lightly edited by me. I made sure to keep the flavor of each composer's speaking style while making necessary corrections in grammar and punctuation in order to give the reader the clearest version of the composer's ideas. Each lecture was then sent to the composer for acceptance, verification, corrections, and additions. They appear in this book in the order in which they were given. Whenever possible, a lecture included a live performance of the lecturer's work, sometimes as a surprise gift.

In my many years of teaching, I have never felt inclined to be inclusive or to survey the entire field of experimental music; rather, I have concentrated on those composers whose music I have loved and admired and who I have felt have broken new ground in defining what music is now or may be in the future. The work of the composers included in this book falls into two broad categories: first, that which more directly follows the spirit and tradition of American experimentalism, from Ives to Cage, and, second, that which takes inspiration from the music of non-

Western cultures, particularly West Africa, Indonesia, and India. Often these two categories overlap.

As the eight composers talked about their work, it became clear that the subjects they talked about, while related to their own music, included an astonishing variety of ideas: the exploration of acoustic phenomena, music of very long duration, talking as music, repetition, pulse, the threshold of audibility, return to tonality, opera for television, the placement and propagation of sound in architectural spaces, song, heterophony, politics, music for the theater, music's place in society and its relationship to popular and world music, the reuse of traditional compositional techniques.

I realize that the term "experimental" is problematic. Many composers hate the term. Edgard Varèse said: "I do not write experimental music. My experimenting is done before I make the music. Afterwards, it is the listener who must experiment."* John Cage, however, describes it as music in which the outcome is uncertain. Works using chance operations or open forms or that set in motion procedures that are neutral in intent may be good examples of the experimental. Some works even resemble experiments in the scientific sense, in that something is discovered during the course of the performance rather than that a preconceived idea or form is brought into being by the will or skill of the composer.

The terms *new* or *contemporary* are too general and may refer to any music of the present. And while it may be radical and even experimental in some way, *avant-garde* refers to a music that merely updates that which precedes it. So, for want of a better word, let us simply accept the term *experimental.*

---

*Edgard Varèse, *The Varèse Album* (LP), New York: Columbia Masterworks, 1972.

John Spencer Camp graduated from Wesleyan in 1878, received a master's degree in 1881, and spent most of his life as a church organist in Hartford, Connecticut. One would think that church organists are conservative by nature, until one remembers that they in fact have to invent and mix their own sounds by choosing from a wide variety of stops, often on extremely large and complex instruments. They are composers, in a way, or at least orchestrators of every piece they play. For that reason, I like to think that while Mr. Camp may not have understood this music entirely, he would have had to admire the skills of the composers in creating their own sounds and putting them together in their works. In 1921, he became CEO of the Austin Organ Company. John Spencer Camp died in 1946.

A person is fortunate to have one good idea in his or her lifetime. Richard K. Winslow, longtime chair of the Wesleyan Music Department and second John Spencer Camp Professor of Music had, in fact, two good ideas. First, along with ethnomusicologist David McAllester, he founded the World Music Department at Wesleyan, an act that changed the teaching of music throughout the world. Wesleyan was the first university music department in which world music was an integral part of the curriculum. Second, very early on, Winslow recognized the genius of John Cage. In 1960, he invited Cage to spend a year at Wesleyan's Center for Advanced Studies and was responsible for the publication of Cage's germinal book, *Silence,* by Wesleyan University Press. Experimental music at Wesleyan (and these lectures) would not have come into existence without Richard Winslow's vision.

Eight Lectures on Experimental Music

1

JAMES TENNEY

April 12, 1989

ALVIN LUCIER

I first came across James Tenney in New York in the 1960s. He, along with Malcolm Goldstein and Philip Corner, had organized the Tone Roads Ensemble (*Tone Roads* is the title of a set of pieces by Charles Ives) that gave concerts of new music. It was wonderful to go to New York and hear the music of John Cage, Edgard Varèse, Henry Cowell, and Morton Feldman. It was the first time we heard this music. Jim played the piano and conducted the ensemble.

Tenney had already made several electronic pieces when he was still in college. One was called *Blue Suede*, a tape collage of the Elvis Presley song. In the early '60s, Jim worked as a resident artist at Bell Labs, in New Jersey, using their computers and making electronic pieces on tape.

In 1967, he gave an influential FORTRAN workshop for a group of composers and Fluxus artists that included Steve Reich, Nam June Paik, Dick Higgins, Jackson Mac Low, Phil Corner, Alison Knowles, and Max Neuhaus. Among his important writings are the seminal *Meta (+) Hodos*, one of earliest applications of gestalt theory and cognitive science to music, as well as *John Cage and the Theory of Harmony*. Nearly a quarter of a 657-page volume of the academic journal *Perspectives of New Music* was devoted to Tenney's music. He also wrote the in-depth liner notes to the Wergo edition of Conlon Nancarrow's *Studies for Player Piano*. (Nancarrow, as a favor, punched the roll for Tenney's *Spectral Canon for Conlon Nancarrow*.) Jim has taught at the Polytechnic Institute of Brooklyn, the University of California at Santa Barbara, and York University in Toronto. He currently teaches at CalArts.

Following the talk, there will be a performance of James Tenney's *The Road to Ubud* for Javanese gamelan and prepared piano. Both Jim and I deeply appreciate the cooperation of my colleagues Mel Strauss, who is going to conduct; John Barlow, who spent hours preparing the piano and discussing the tunings; Sumarsam, director of the Wesleyan gamelan, who helped us examine the tuning of the gamelan; and also all of the students who have so generously given their time. I am delighted to introduce James Tenney, the first John Spencer Camp lecturer in music.

JAMES TENNEY

When I was asked a month or so ago what I would talk about, I couldn't come to any clear decision. I thought I might just talk about recent works. But I think that what I would like to do is talk about harmony, using a few examples from pieces of mine as a kind of elaborate preparation for hearing my piece for gamelan and prepared piano.

When I say harmony, I don't mean what you may think I mean. I don't mean triadic, diatonic, common-practice harmony, although I would like to think that that could be a subset of what harmony might eventually come to mean for us. That would be one particular manifestation of it. I have felt for some time, in fact, I guess for almost twenty years, that a concern for harmony has been important in the music that I was writing in a variety of different ways, and I've also tried to deal with these questions theoretically. Now, it remains to be seen, and we won't know for some time whether I've accomplished anything in this respect, but I have some ideas that I would like to talk with you about before you hear this piece.

One is a view of what's happened in music in the twentieth century, a sort of historical viewpoint. It seems to me that harmony as a functional part of music was evolving, changing quite noticeably in Western music in the eighteenth and nineteenth centuries. From one period to another, we can hear changes in this respect, and I think the notion of an evolution is not unrealistic. But by the end of the nineteenth century, and certainly by about 1910, the first decade of the twentieth century, something strange seems to have happened. It's as though the more progressive composers got to a point where they felt that the evolution of harmony had reached an impasse, a dead end where, for some reason, it couldn't evolve any further. Now, being irrepressible, creative musicians weren't about to stop making music, so what happened is they went off into a number of different directions investigating other aspects of music: rhythm, tone quality, texture, form, even the social function and aesthetics of music. All of these different aspects began to be investigated in a way that has resulted in an incredible body of beautiful exciting music. The legacy of this century is as rich as any previous century in Western history. But, harmony as such, it has seemed to me for a long time, never got beyond the point it had reached in about 1910.

A few years ago, I decided to go back and see if there were

some way that we could take that sense of an evolutionary impasse in harmony as a challenge and move with it without simply regressing to some earlier stage. I don't mean anything "neo" by this, but I am concerned with "can we move on, forward" with this? And I hope I have also made it clear that this is in no way a criticism of music that I would maintain was not doing anything with harmony. All right?

One thing that occurred to me was that maybe our very understanding of the word *harmony* was problematic. It's very interesting to think about what the word had come to mean and compare it to its earlier historical meaning. Facts arise from that. In early Greece, the meaning of the word that is the root of our word *harmony* meant something as simple and general as "a fitting together of things," like two stones shaped to fit snugly or two pieces of wood pressed together to form a unit. The Pythagoreans adopted the term and extended it to mean things very broadly philosophical and religious, but still it meant the way things relate to one another in the cosmos. And in their application of that concept to music, it is my understanding that what they had in mind was the way in which different pitches related to each other. It had nothing to do with necessarily sounding those pitches together. In fact, there is some question that they ever considered the sounds together. In any case, that was not primarily what they were talking about. They meant the relationships between different pitches.

The Pythagoreans discovered some wonderful things: for example, that certain strings produced tones that were in simple harmonic relationships to each other. Eventually, the meaning of the word got narrowed, restricted more and more. If you look at current dictionary definitions it will be something about the vertical structure of music. It's even more restricted than that: chords. Even more restricted than that: triads, with maybe a few added notes here and there. It got narrowed down, and to me the epitome of that process of narrowing is something that may not be completely universal terminology in the jazz world, but I have heard it. Certain instruments are melody instruments, others are rhythm instruments or harmony instruments, meaning the obvious thing: a harmony instrument is one that can play more than two pitches at a single time.

This is so restrictive, especially if this is carried even further, simply to mean triads. If we had to accept that idea, it would surely be the case that there was nowhere to go. I wouldn't even be interested in harmony in that sense. But I don't think it is necessary to leave it that restricted. I wouldn't advocate going back to Pythagorean generalities either. They're a little too broad. I think it can usefully be defined as having to do with certain types of relations between pitches.

One of the areas that I first began to investigate in my pieces was the acoustical phenomenon that had to do with the harmonic series. You probably all know something about the presence of the harmonic series in sustained tones. I did a number of pieces in which the composition itself was based more or less directly upon the harmonic series. Now I want to play a couple of tapes of short pieces that explore these phenomena. The first one is called *Septet*. It's written for six electric guitars and electric bass. You will hear a gradual unfolding, or sort of extension up the harmonic series to a certain point, and then a narrowing down of the range toward the top of that series, at which point it begins to open up again in a different series. It's all very straightforward, but it's kind of fun when you hear it on electric guitars.

Now, with the earlier works in the 1970s, I allowed for some pretty casual tunings. But by this time, I made every effort to get precise tunings from the instruments. The fretted strings of guitars had to be adjusted to get the necessary precision. Because the harmonic series, those natural intervals, are noticeably different from tempered intervals, the open strings of the guitars were tuned in such a way that, when they played the frets needed to get those pitches, the pitches were pretty accurate. The same is the case here with the prepared piano.

There's another work that again uses the harmonic series as a basic feature. No special tuning is involved because I was able to make use of a natural musical phenomenon. It's a piece for viola, cello, string bass, and a tape delay system. The three instruments produce what are called harmonic glissandi on the strings: simply moving the left hand, the finger touching lightly, up and down the length of the string. In the course of the piece, it's actually a canon in three voices, you'll hear the three voices, and if you know it's a canon, maybe you will hear those relationships. The bass is tuned in fifths an octave below the cello. So it's a canon at the octave using harmonic glissandi, beginning on the C strings; then moving gradually up with canonic delays to the G, D, and A strings; and then finally cascading back down. So you have that kind of very consonant sounding situation toward the beginning where everything comes from the harmonic series on C. But pretty soon that gets to be a little more complicated. This is the first movement of a longer work. The whole piece is called *Glissade*, and this movement is called "Shimmer."

One can't go on indefinitely writing pieces based on the harmonic series, but I learned a number of useful things from this work. Some of them are quite obvious. One is that the lower-order harmonics tend to be easily understood by our ears as consonant. The higher we go in the series, particularly with the prime number harmonic partials, the more complex the relationships become—and in some ways the more dissonant the relationships may be perceived to be. I also learned that when various pitches of a given harmonic series, that is, a series over a given fundamental, are heard together, the ear has a remarkable ability to fuse them into a singular, unified percept. This must be the case because virtually every sustained tone we ever hear, including vowels of the singing voice, are actually complex combinations of the individual pitches. It is because they are in this particular relationship that our ears hear them as a singular thing. And it has seemed to me, for some time, that this is an important insight because any theory of harmony, if it's to be developed, tells us something about how we perceive. It would be a theory of harmonic perception, not of harmonic practice.

Now, this also threw some new light on the historical viewpoint that I was talking about in relation to the evolution of harmony in the nineteenth century and the impasse that was reached in 1910 but by way of another insight, or perhaps a hypothesis. I'll put it to you as that. I think our ears interpret intervals of any kind as though they were the nearest simple interval in this kind of harmonic series relationship. That is, we even hear even intervals that are out of tune as more or less distorted versions of simple intervals. By simple, I should say also "natural," as they occur in the harmonic series. By the way, if we have any part of nature that we can pick to use in our music, that's it. Everything else is culture, style, and psychology. The harmonic series is physics.

Anyway, my hypothesis is that whatever intervals we hear, we interpret them, more or less, as distorted versions of a certain set of relatively simple intervals. This is the way tempered tuning systems are acceptable to us. It becomes important to understand what the twelve-tone temperament, which we have been living with for so long, is. It was a fairly good approximation of a set of important natural intervals. The deviations, the distortions, were considered to be acceptable and worth the price that one had to pay to achieve certain things like endless modulation and so forth, the ability to repeat the same melodic idea in another key region and not move into impossible regions. The impasse that was reached in 1910 was determined precisely by the fact that the twelve-tone temperament was designed to approximate a certain limited set of harmonic relations. Music had been based on those relations for a couple hundred years, and the evolution of harmony couldn't go any further with that tuning system. This implies that if we want to keep going, we have to start looking at other tuning systems.

One of the things that was done around that time was the subdivision of the twelve tones into quarter tones or sixth tones. This didn't get very far, however, because quarter tones don't really get any closer to those important harmonic relations than semitones do. They didn't help much. I think what needs to be done is experimenting with a variety of different tuning systems, and if what we're interested in is harmony, we have to design them to have harmonic effects.

A recent work of mine makes use of another temperament containing equal divisions of the octave into not twelve but seventy-two parts, so that the smallest interval is one-sixth of a semitone. For those of you who know acoustical terminology, about seventeen cents is the smallest interval one can hear. It is for acoustic instruments. The way I did this, if you can believe it, was to get six harps together. (It's a beautiful sight on one stage.) Within each harp, the tuning is the normal tempered tuning, but the harps are tuned a sixth of a semitone apart. The piece was written as though for one enormous superharp. It's extremely difficult because everyone is playing just one-sixth of the whole part. But it worked out. The reason I chose that one is that that subdivision gives extremely good approximations to all of the natural intervals that I was interested in. It does an awfully good job of approximating them. The work is called *Changes*. It is a series of short studies for six harps, based on a number of lines that make up a hexagram in the *I Ching*. I used a computer in the composition process. The textures are stochastically generated and controlled. Each of the pieces is named after one of the hexagrams of the *I Ching*. I am going to play just three of them for you. Each of them is about two minutes long. The first is called "Holding Together," the second, "Duration," and the third, "Difficulty at the Beginning."

One of the implications of our use of any tempered system or any approximation of those simpler, what I'm calling "natural," intervals we find in the harmonic series is that the ear must have a certain tolerance range for those approximations. If we interpret a given interval as something slightly different, then there must be a range in which this interpretation is possible. And that notion of tolerance is an extremely important one that has to be brought into any debate about the use of just intervals, just tuning systems, and so forth. Too often the people who have arguments about that seem, on the one side, to imply that any mistuning at all is unacceptable. But, in fact, we live in a world where we never get anything perfect. As far as I am concerned, these tiles in the floor are perfectly square. But, if we get down there with calipers and measure them very precisely, we discover that they are all slightly different. So, the twelve-tone tempered system is a useful one for certain kinds of music and for certain kinds of harmony.

Now, I am going to claim that the five-tone Pelog scale in Javanese music is also useful for a certain kind of harmony. I don't think there is much precedent for that in the literature. I'm assuming—well, I'd better be careful now, I'm surrounded by musicologists. Don't take whatever I say as a musicological hypothesis, but as a composer's working assumption. I am going to tell you about the piece that you are going to hear tonight. My assumption here was that the Pelog tuning, which for those of you that are not familiar with it, let me let you hear it on one of these instruments. [Plays.] We hear, first of all, three pitches separated by small intervals, then a larger interval, another small interval, then a large one.

That set of pitches can be approximated by a series of small intervals by a circle of small fifths. What do I mean by small fifths? In the twelve-tone temperament, our fifths are small but only by a fiftieth of a semitone. They're two cents smaller than the natural interval. If we use a smaller interval of 667 cents, a third of a semitone small, and try to make a circle of these, it will in fact make a circle that will repeat itself after nine pitches. It's a nine-tone equal division of the octave. But if you take the first five of them, they create a configuration that is extremely close to the Pelog scale.

Whether there is any genetic relationship there I have no way of knowing. I decided to tune the piano to a nine-tone equal division and then adjust the piano's actual absolute frequency level so that it could best fit with the pitches of the gamelan. The gamelan ensemble can only play a set of five tones at that level of the piano; however, the same scale structure can be reproduced at each of the nine pitches. What I just played is very close to this. What happens in the piece is that there is a continual modulation, in fact, just similar to what we might find in Western tonal music—modulation by descending small fifths. So, the music as a whole is moving around that circle of fifths that has nine steps to it. In the whole twenty minutes of the piece that circle is gone through six times. At the beginning, only the piano can play all the five pitches in the Pelog, based on the initial basic tone. The gamelan can only play one of them. So, you'll hear the gamelan every once in a while, punctuating the piano sounds with these same pitches. Then another one comes in when the piano begins to modulate. Eventually, the piano will have gone through that series to a point where its five pitches correspond precisely to the five pitches that can be played by the gamelan. So it becomes kind of a concerto form, in a way, with more activity in the piano and waves of activity on the gamelan.

Originally, the first idea about this piece had to do with just the timbre. It's remarkable that preparing a piano string in certain ways reminds lots of people of the sounds of the metallophones in the gamelan. I was commissioned to write a piece for a small gamelan group in Toronto, which will help explain the rather pathetic underuse of this magnificent set of instruments that you see before you. I've only got six players up here. More than half of the resources on that stage are being wasted, which I regret considerably because I would think it would be an absolutely magnificent sound if I used every one of them.

The piece was composed using a computer in the composition process. I'm always very careful to put it that way because I don't want anybody to think that my computer composed the piece. I composed it, but my computer was a very useful tool in working out various aspects of it. The process is something that I call stochastic. I'm using that term in a slightly different way than Xenakis did. Very simply it means "a constrained, random process." Constrained by various kinds of shape functions that direct it. It's never completely free. And that's it. Are all the players here? If they are ready, I'm ready.

2

CHRISTIAN WOLFF

April 24, 1990

ALVIN LUCIER

I first met Christian Wolff in the late 1950s in Cambridge, Massachusetts. At that time he was a tutor in classics at Harvard. From time to time he organized concerts of new music at Kirkland House, all-day affairs that included works of John Cage, David Behrman, Gordon Mumma, Frederic Rzewski, myself, and others, as well as films by Tony Conrad.

In 1965, when I invited John Cage to perform a concert in the Rose Art Museum at Brandeis, where I was teaching at the time, John suggested that we include a work of Christian's. I was delighted to do so. In that concert, John, Christian, and I performed his *for 1, 2 or 3 people*, an early signature piece that used cuing as a way to produce indeterminate results.

Many of you know this work; I include it in Music 109, Introduction to Experimental Music. It is a democratic idea—a player not having to be a prodigious performer but one who requires an acutely aware social attitude toward performance. Amateurs as well as professionals share the stage. I have often thought of Christian's works for small ensembles as a perfect form of chamber music; each player depends on the playing of the others. Following Christian's lecture, three of our graduate students will perform this work as a surprise gift to Christian.

Artists and composers, as well as scientists and engineers, often stumble upon great new ideas. I have often thought that innovative or shocking ideas in art—cubism in painting, for example—do not come about through deep analytical thought on the part of the artist but come about by accident, in the actual or whimsical process of working on a painting or musical composition. One story goes that Picasso was so upset with his then mistress that he drew a distorted picture of her by moving her nose to one side. Christian's breakthrough technique of cuing among players came about as he was working on a piece for two pianists. He was running out of time and needed to finish the piece for an upcoming performance, so he developed this shorthand notation. This solution to a practical problem became a philosophical idea in his subsequent music.

By the early '70s, Christian decided to write in a more traditional style, in order to make his music more accessible to everyday musicians. For several years I have struggled to figure out where his earlier ideas of indeterminate processes might be lurking in his more traditional notation. Perhaps one answer lies in the quirkiness of the narrative, the syntax and grammar of the flow of his pieces. Often one phrase doesn't seem to follow logically from what came just before; it seems totally unrelated. The choice of instruments in many of his works is free and sometimes produces strange bedfellows. During visits to art colleges in England in the '70s, he made a series of prose scores for nonmusicians. Students in Music 109 are well acquainted with *Stones*, which we perform in class every year. "Make sounds with stones, draw sounds out of stones, using a number of sizes and kinds . . ."

Christian's approach to political works is direct and gentle. He often uses texts and workers' songs, sometimes hidden in the texture of a work, similar to the use of folk music by other American composers, including Aaron Copland. Many are about women (Rosa Parks, Rosa Luxemburg, Harriet Tubman, the female workers in a shirt factory in Lowell, Massachusetts). He quotes from songs of Holly Near.

When European composers visit Wesleyan, they often ask to go to three places in New England: Union Cemetery in nearby Killingworth, to visit Hermann Broch's grave; Concord, Massachusetts, to visit Henry Thoreau's cabin on Walden Pond; and Hanover, New Hampshire, to visit Christian Wolff, who currently teaches music and classics at Dartmouth College. Tonight, he is here in Middletown, Connecticut, to talk to you in person. The title of his lecture is "What Is Our Work?"

CHRISTIAN WOLFF

Thank you, Alvin.

What is our work? What I mean is, What are we—composers, producers of music—doing and, perhaps, what should we be doing? I also mean, how are we doing it?

Who are we? Well, I'll have to speak mostly for myself, if only because I have more of the material at hand, than for anyone else. But I've said *we* and *our* because the musical enterprise is inevitably social or, if you will, political, in one way or another. We all need to survive materially to start with, and our work, whatever it is, will be affected by that, while our material survival obviously depends on social networks. (For example, the extraordinary character of John Cage's work in [the] 1950s and early '60s, the alarming and beautiful blend in it of power and danger—in addition to, almost in spite of, the music's refusal of rhetoric—must owe something to his continuously endangered economic life at the time. Over roughly the same period, Elliott Carter, in total economic security, evolved his characteristically hypercomplex and hyperdeterminate hermetic music. Somewhere in between, a larger number of us have been employed by universities and colleges: How has that affected our work?)

Apart from this aspect of the material environment in which we work, there is the wider social one of an economy geared to mass consumption, on the one hand, and therefore to a homogenizing of our cultural experience, and, on the other hand, an economy that feeds on a privatizing technology: recordings, Walkmans, videos, VCRS, all are for individual, private use because no doubt more will be sold if everyone is persuaded that he or she must have this equipment, or, indeed, they must have it if they want any access to the main currents of the culture. In this way, the technology is antisocial and objectifies cultural products, makes them consumer items, and so suppresses the liveliness they might have in a particular social setting of audience and performer(s). Of course, technology can be useful and mind-stretching; it's a human creation, and it's extended extraordinarily access to both cultural products and cultural work. In music, for instance, if you can get hold of or construct or modify equipment, with some intelligence and with information that is more or less available, you can make music, and you can do it in ways that may alter notions of what music might be. Technology, too, may offer means of us for our making connections between popular and so-called art music.

I also refer to our work in the plural because, though I know rather less of other music that's being made than I would like, I try to think about it, respond to it in some way in my own work. At times, I have worked closely with—and performed with—others, and that's affected my work: for instance, David Tudor, John Cage, Frederic Rzewski, Cornelius Cardew, Gordon Mumma, the members of the English improvising group AMM, John Tilbury, Garrett List. Other musics have affected me all my life. Some musics I admire and don't know what to do about it, but because they exist I have the feeling that they allow me to get on with what I am doing: for example, the music of Nancarrow, Tudor, Oliveros, Lucier, Nono, Ashley, Feldman. As for the other musics that have affected my work, I should mention that they include musics of the past, Western classical music (on much of which I was raised from an early age), going back to the medieval period; musics of other traditions—African Ba-Benzele Pygmy, for instance; and some jazz (for example, Ornette Coleman)—and I have drawn, for musical material, considerably from folk music, particularly North American and black and politically connected.

All these musics could be called "influences," although, except for the use of tunes (from political folk music), there is no deliberate, conscious use of them, no effort to adapt or imitate. In many cases, I think of them after the fact of my own writing, as though having come away from a conversation with them (or one or more parts of them). I carry on the talk on my own, and perhaps they are listening. They can also provide a kind of corroboration and encouragement. While working on the first set of *Exercises*, which are mostly single- or double-pitch lines to be played by a variable number of unspecified instruments in a freely heterophonic way, for example, I happened to hear part of a performance of the thirteenth-century *Cantigas de Santa Maria*, which sounded to me at once various, rich, and clear; and then I found out that it was all based on a single notated pitch line. After making the piece *Stones* (a prose instruction for an improvisation using stones as the basic sound source), I brought a copy of it to Cornelius Cardew, who, when he had looked at it, reached over and handed me his score-in-progress of *The Great Learning*, paragraph 1, in which members of a chorus must make sounds with stones, according to a graphic notation based on Chinese characters. Cornelius had thought to use stones because, beautifully cut and tuned, they are often used in Chinese classical music. My piece had originally come about after a long afternoon on a stone-covered beach, discovering and trying out the range of sounds that a variety of stones are capable of producing. In the case of each of these pieces, you could say an area of community of interest was discovered and identified. With the *Cantigas*, initially a formal procedure—heterophony and flexible instrumental realization—was shared, but, then too, some of the conditions underlying this way of making the music: collaborative performance (nonhierarchical), the mix of popular and so-called high cultural elements (the *Cantigas* draw widely from folk tunes; the *Exercises* are full of diatonic bits; both require a more-than-simply-popular formality of performance presentation). In the case of *Stones*, common interests in the exploration of new (or so we thought) sound sources intersected, coming in the one case from a piece's content—*The Great Learning* sets texts of Confucius—and in the other from experiment with natural objects.

I think of the contemporary musical work I have referred to and my own work as experimental. What does that mean? Or what can we suggest it usefully to mean?

It's first of all partly a question of circumstances, as with the related notion of "new music." That is, it's a sliding notion. The earliest new music I know about appeared at the end of the fifth century before Christ in Athens (people complained at the time that it undermined the traditional modes or "harmonies"; that it misused, by extending them, instrumental techniques; that it was directionless—zigzagging about like ants—and rhythmically unstable; that it obscured the words of texts which it set; that it corrupted the young). In the early fourteenth century, a "new art," *ars nova*, of music (or, more precisely, of musical notation) was identified. And so forth down the centuries. And evidently by the beginning of the twentieth century, the beginnings of "our" new music emerged, most characteristically, it seemed, around the figure of Schoenberg. By the mid-1950s, one of Schoenberg's greatest apologists, Theodor W. Adorno, wrote about the "aging new (modern) music," a powerful essay in which he claimed that this aging was due to the fact that "the young no longer dared to be young." By the late '60s (shortly before his death), he wrote, more generally, and perhaps more suggestively, that "the new [in art] is the longing for the new, not the new itself."

Adorno follows up this observation by remarking that modern art (or twentieth-century music), identifying itself as new, assumes a notion of progress, assumes that the new constitutes an improvement on the old. Yet, he also observes, the world around us doesn't seem to be improving; it is, in fact, in a state of extraordinary crisis—the gap between rich and poor, violence, the use of torture, the abuse of the environment are reaching unprecedented proportions (I update his examples somewhat). If, then, Adorno argues, art would be linked with progress, it must represent a utopian impulse, an expression or image of, or desire for, a better world. But such a representation, insofar as "social reality increasingly impedes Utopia," will implicate art in the fostering of delusion and false comfort, will make it a lie.

There are, of course, more familiar notions of the new. Bach, you remember, had to provide a new cantata every Sunday—which recalls that the idea of performing old music, of musical reruns, is relatively recent (and as it happened, Bach was one of its first beneficiaries). Nowadays when you use the term *new music*, it can mean what is currently on the pop charts or refer to groups just emerging on the scene, whatever their musical style or sound happens to be. Here the new is associated with novelty, with what is fashionable, up-to-date, not yet passé, an association easily connected to marketing strategies looking to extend and expand consumption.

There is a beautiful moment early in Homer's *Odyssey* (we are back in the early eighth century before Christ) in which Odysseus's wife, Penelope, asks the singer who is entertaining unwelcome guests in her house not to sing the heartbreaking song of her husband's absence. Her son, Telemachus, however, checks her, saying, "Why, my mother, do you begrudge this excellent singer / his pleasing himself as the thought drives him? It is not the singers / who are to blame, it must be Zeus [the all-powerful of the gods] is to blame, who gives out / to men who eat bread, to each and all, the way he wills it. / There is nothing wrong in his singing the sad return of the Danaans [the Greeks, including Odysseus]. / People, surely, always give more applause to that song / which is the latest to circulate among the listeners." And he continues, "So let your heart and let your spirit be hardened to listen. Odysseus is not the only one who lost his homecoming / day at Troy. There were many others who perished, besides him." The passage is beautiful in part because of its intricacies: we (the audience) know, in fact, that Odysseus has not lost his homecoming but is on his way, and the song from which this passage is taken, the "Odyssey," is the song of that homecoming, which will complete, or continue, the new but in fact not-yet-completed song, which is so painful to Penelope and which Telemachus defends on the grounds of its newness. He also defends the new song on the grounds of the singer's inspiration, or need to sing what he sings; on the grounds that the song represents reality (what Zeus has dispensed), which affects a far larger group than just Odysseus—though, as said, Telemachus misapprehends some of that reality; and on the grounds that the present company (however unwelcome and threatening they happen to be) has a claim on the song's newness that outweighs consideration of the private grief it causes Penelope.

We might mention in passing that the performance of orally transmitted and of improvised musics, which are in many cases traditional musics, is always, strictly speaking, new. Such performance, one could say, exists only for the present, albeit in some cases as a kind of foreground on that particular music's traditional background.

When all is said and done, we need and want, in some sense that matters, what is new. What will it be? How will it be determined?

Before continuing with those questions, I'd like to suggest a schematic outline of how one might see the need for what is new. Under one general heading of subjective or personal there is (1) an appetite for novelty somehow in each of us; and (2) another way of seeing that appetite, as at once the ineluctable fact of our individual, continual changing, becoming always new, growing and decaying, and our individual desire, variously and activated, to grow, change, renovate, change our skins—it is a matter of reminding ourselves that we are alive. The second general heading I would label objective or social and locate there; (3) the capitalist market economy, driven by the need for continuing and increasing profits and intent, with all the resources of mass communication, on exciting in us unending desires for its products and services; and (4) the larger condition of the world and its crises (some of whose manifestations were mentioned earlier), crying out for change and transformation. All four of these elements interpenetrate; all of them are either changeable or capable of instigating change.

Of course we have deep needs for stability and gentle continuity. Change is work and can be scary as well as exhilarating. And there are always those who have, or imagine themselves to have, some advantage of power or privilege and who will resist change by every means, including in the extreme case, their own destruction. In fact, stability is not a given, not a choice as such.

It, too, has constantly to be re-created through the processes of change. As for the notion that there is nothing new under the sun, while sobering, it seems to me useless, all too conducive to inertia and passive resignation.

Now, what about music? It seems to me that everything said so far about the new and about change points to experimental music. Not, of course, that music as such will somehow save us. Obviously there are enormous gaps between social and musical problems. But they are also linked, a linking that at the very least urges us to take our musical problems seriously.

What is experimental? In some ways it is, as said before, a variable notion, differently realized at different times or by different works. The word suggests something that you don't know how it's going to turn out. It can have an apologetic sound to it—"this is only an experiment"—implying a displacement of the real thing, or that one is only on the way, more or less groping, toward the real thing, that the point is to establish something else, more important, on a firm foundation: to prove it. From this I would eliminate the apologetic tone but retain the suggestion of exploration. I would also put on hold the notion that there is something out there that we can ultimately prove. Experiment implies working amidst the unknown. It acknowledges the unknown, respects it, but is not frightened by it. Experiment should be such as to involve genuine risk, that is, truly acknowledging the unknown in which it operates, and so establish its seriousness.

One way to consider the experimental character of music is to notice its effect on listeners (though I don't want to stress this point: as a composer, I'm more concerned with production than reception; though of course I'm not indifferent to the latter, but consideration of it doesn't enter into the actual processes of making my work, except to the extent that it might allow listeners to be free to do their own listening). Effects such as surprise, shock, astonishment, irritation, boredom, bemusement, I find this very difficult to talk about, but I thought it should be mentioned. One of the most encouraging things I have heard said about my work was that although this person didn't really like what she was hearing, the performance of the music made her feel that she wanted to be a musician. David Behrman once said after a concert that he liked the music because it was honest and it was funny (humorous).

I would like to think of bemusement as a good result of this music, bemusement at what was heard, mixed in with, variously, pleasure, perhaps exhilaration, and bemusement in the mind, waking it up also to the social world around it. Of course music—experimental music—may be allowed a variety of functions. Henry Brant thinks of music as "medicine for the spirit."

Let me give you an example of how context can affect the experimental character of a piece of music. In 1975, I was asked to provide music for a Merce Cunningham Company "event," one of those evening-long performances put together out of material from various dances. As usual, no specifications were indicated about the music except for the total length of time within which it could take place. No information was provided about the character of the dance. Merce Cunningham's work is of course experimental, and part of that experimentalism is to allow the music that accompanies the dance to be itself rather than an accompaniment. The music that I provided included a new piece that used material from a song, originally a popular song of the 1920s (I think) called "Redwing," which was later (in 1940) adapted by Woodie Guthrie to make a political song called "Union Maid." We—the musicians (there were four of us altogether)—decided to include in the performance a singing of "Union Maid." Not, I may say, without some previous anxious deliberation. At any rate, the song, roughly sung (none of us were polished singers), coming at a point in the dance—unpredictably—where Merce

Cunningham was performing one of his beautiful solos, was shocking (I even remember hearing the odd gasp from the audience). An ordinary, perky tune was shocking in a context that routinely absorbed musics like John Cage's, David Tudor's, Pauline Oliveros's, Alvin Lucier's, and, for that matter, my own. My sense of what might constitute an experimental music performance has never been the same.

The usual view is that experimental music is distinguished by the presence of new sound or (and) new ways of arranging sound and (or), we might add, new contexts (which might well be social) for sounds. (As another example of the latter, consider the performance by some of New York's best players, members of the Philharmonic, et cetera, of Mozart's woodwind quintet at a concert sponsored by the Musicians' Action Collective, a politically oriented organization, as a benefit for the Farm Workers' Union, a concert including political folk music, jazz, and new music and attended by an audience including the various followers of these musics, most of whom were also supporters of the farm workers' cause. Mozart's piece in this context became a political piece in, I would claim, a new, experimental way.)

Something of the feeling of this newness is also suggested by John Cage's remark that "the trick is suddenly to appear in a place without apparent means of transport." More explicitly, Cage has also insisted that the essential meaning of *experimental* is unpredictability. He urges work of such a kind that its realization (sometimes as a musical composition, sometimes as a performance, sometimes both) will surprise the one who made it, in some cases the one(s) who perform it, and, in a rather different way, those who listen. In the case of those who listen, the sense of hearing something surprising is different because they don't really know the conditions of the experiment—the experimental conditions of a particular work. If a certain sound has been arrived at by chance (either in the composition process or the performing), how can you tell just from hearing it? To be sure, if the sound is unlike any you have heard before, you will appreciate its experimental character; but you do so in the context of all your experience of listening to music; and if you should hear this sound again, it will, in this view, cease to be experimental. Well, perhaps. The example of the single sound is a bit overly simple. The experimental character of a piece, as it involves unpredictability (and not necessarily just new sounds), is more likely to be found in the way the piece makes its own context: the piece as a whole may or may not seem new or surprising, but it will create a setting within which its surprises take place. You could think of background (the piece as a whole) and foreground (the things that affect you as surprise). It may also be that foreground and background—surprisingly—change into one another.

To return to John Cage just once more, he has a reason for stressing the notion of unpredictability. It's to allow you, the listener, but also himself and the players to be more alert and attentive in this way: the unpredictability is a result or symptom of compositional techniques (in his case the use of chance in the process of composing and sometimes in the overlaying of independent individual performers' parts or of several independently made compositions for a given performance), techniques intended to free up the music from extramusical pressures, such as the desire to express a feeling or idea or image or whatever, even the desire to be beautiful. This is not to say that such expressions might not appear or be felt by listeners to appear, but the point is that they would appear without specific intention: they would take you by surprise, innocently and without compulsion. Allowing each of us individually to be free in this way is the utopian element in such a view of experimental music. (It has also a kind of practical realism about it, insofar as there is almost inevitably—especially in times so culturally heterogeneous as ours—a gap between the expressive intention behind a work and how its listeners (variously) understand it. The absence of specific expressive intent would preclude misunderstanding about such an intent, or, to put it in another way, such an absence allows a work expressive flexibility.

When I began composing, I had the notion—I don't really know where it came from, perhaps an adolescent impulse—that I should make a music unlike any other. I was encouraged too by hearing for the first time, after a long immersion in the older Western classical music (roughly from Bach to Brahms), the string quartet music of Bartók, Berg, Schoenberg, and Webern. (This was in 1949, when opportunities for hearing this music even in New York were very rare and no recordings were available.) The music, especially in its sonorities, the kinds of noise it made, its continuities, its dissonances, felt extraordinarily bracing and like nothing I had encountered before and, by virtue of this, liberating. I wanted, in my way, to do the same. And for the next twenty or so years, this is what I tried to do, making a music that whatever else might be said about it, could be called experimental in the senses of that word suggested so far. But in the early '70s, something caught up with me. Like many people at that time—and they included a number of musicians with whom I worked—I was (to make a longer story short and simple) politicized, and for the first time I thought about the connections between my emerging political concerns and my musical work (earlier involvement with pacifism and civil rights activity had had no such effect). My previous work now seemed to me too esoteric and, because of its performance requirements—involving the players in a kind of exclusive, intense concentration on each other's sounds—too introverted: the gap between the performers' involvement with a piece's sound and the listeners' seemed too large. What I was doing musically seemed mostly inaccessible to people (including good friends) who were, generally speaking, music lovers.

My first response was to attach to my music texts that were political in character or implication. As I said earlier, social arrangements find, in one form or another, representation in music (as in any kind of human activity), either implicitly or unconsciously or explicitly or consciously. It could be said that my work shifted from an implicit expression of the politics of a kind of democratic libertarianism akin to anarchism to an explicit politics of, roughly speaking, democratic socialism. And, in the music, I tried to make my work less introverted, less sparse, more of a response to what a larger number of people might recognize as music.

What, now, has happened to the notion of experiment?

The combinations of sounds (not quite the sounds themselves) may have something new about them, but the way they are put together also draws on more familiar procedures. In the earlier *Pairs* (1969), for instance, there is hardly a trace of usual musical techniques, at most a variant of hocketing (sharing out a melody line, mostly note by note, between two or more players) but without fixed rhythmic definition; perhaps something like counterpoint in the overlaying of paired players but without any specific motivic relationships—fragments of melody. No system is used in the note-to-note procedure of composing. Perhaps most important (though of course everything is important), the composing involved working out the conditions under which something I would regard as musical, a process, would be able to take place, conditions allowing a high degree of variability in timing and in density of sound.

John Cage used to remark that he found my work musical (this was not a value judgment); after a rehearsal of *Bowery Preludes*, Garrett List said to me, "Don't get this wrong, I really like these pieces: they're so unmusical." Morton Feldman was heard to say that the writing was idiomatic and unidiomatic. The making of *Pairs* could be said to have spun itself out of itself (but I also think there is something of Webern in the background, though not in any of the technical procedures). *Bowery Preludes* from 1987 uses counterpoint—the piccolo and trombone duet, for instance, is a kind of two-part invention; there is identifiable melodic hocketing; there are longer patches of clear rhythmic articulation (as far as pitch is concerned, the earlier work starts with the assumption of complete chromaticism but has plenty of room for the appearance of diatonic moments, while the later starts with diatonic material, which easily shifts in and out of chromaticism; noise is always a possibility in both cases; I'm tempted to say that the nondecorative presence of noise is one of the clearest identifying features of experimental music—and I'd be willing to extend the notion of noise to the way sound appears in, say, Nancarrow or Lucier or even Feldman).

Behind these differences in the more recent work (actually, the work of about the last seventeen years) is the technical—and more-than-technical—fact that the music in many cases draws its material from songs, most of them not my own but a variety of political songs or folk songs or black spirituals, which have had or have acquired association with political or social issues: for instance, in *Bowery Preludes* use is made of the spirituals "Mary, Don't You Weep," "Oh, Freedom," and "Set Down, Servant," all songs originally expressing, under religious guise, the Southern slaves' aspirations to freedom and then taken up again during the Civil Rights movement in the 1960s (I first heard "Mary, Don't You Weep" on a highly political Staple Singers album in the early '70s). Also used are a black prison song, "Ain't No Mo' Cane on Dis Brazos," first sung by slaves in the cane fields on the Brazos River in Texas and apparently still sung by the mostly black prison population hired out to this day to work in those same fields, and a contemporary British women's "Picket Line Song," written during an equal-pay strike in London in 1976. I should mention that one part of *Bowery Preludes* uses no such song material and is notated in such a way as to focus the players entirely on dynamics and sonority.

The way the song material may be used varies, but mostly the pitch intervals and the rhythms are variously represented, transformed, augmented, diminished, extended by additive processes, and so forth. The song is rarely quoted directly. (There are affinities here with Ives, for instance, and the English keyboard music of the turn of the seventeenth century.) The songs—which I choose not just for their political content but also because I really like them as songs—also provide a kind of guiding spirit to the composing. It's not that I set out to express in the music the content of the song (the words would then, in any case, be necessary). Rather, as, for example, in the trombone and piccolo duet in *Bowery Preludes*, the partly humorous militancy of the "Picket Line Song" is both in the musical material in my hands, so to speak, being variously modified, and in my head as I work, as a kind of wider-structure or scaffolding of feeling, which is not really the same thing as setting out to make a piece intended to express humorous militancy (about, incidentally, a quite serious issue).

Now, what has happened to the notion of *experimental* as a way of working that is free of specific or directed expressive intentions? Perhaps not so much. Generally speaking, of course, I believe my earlier and later music sound different (though there is still sometimes that thread of noise running between them). But in each—earlier underlying, later perhaps more on the surface, earlier in the way the sounds are made, later more in what the sounds refer to—there is a concern about freedom. I don't want to make any easy metaphorical jump from musical to political or even personal freedom; but if we believe that our music is part of our larger social existence, then some such connection, however flickering, may be there. It is also the case that every work, no matter how indeterminate or experimental, has its particular expressive horizons, even when what is expressed is the freedom of sounds to be just sounds: that freedom is a signified meaning made by us, not by the sounds. The expressive possibilities of, say, *Pairs* are delimited—only a certain range of expression or meaning could imaginably be found in them, experienced because of them, a range that can be identified, though you may not be able to put it into words. (These remarks are, of course, in no way value judgments.) Every piece, I think, has—in addition to the abstract arrangement of its sounds or simply the existence of its sounds and their possible relation to whatever other sounds are going on around them—what I would call a content, something that it suggests, which is not the same as its sounds, though such a content may deeply affect those sounds, how they are arranged and how they appear to us. For example, in Cage, that content has often to do with nature, stars, the seasons, plants, or the words of Thoreau. All this affects how we hear the sounds in his music, how their horizon of expressiveness is indicated. In *Pairs*, the content could be said to have something to do with working together, two by two. In my more recent work that content often relates to a political mood: assertive, resistant, commemorative, celebrative, for instance. The connection may be fairly tenuous or subterranean; it is often discontinuous. As for indeterminacy, it will always exist in some form; it's our destiny, because we're mortal. The trick is not to forget it. In the recent music I've been speaking about, one could say that that indeterminacy is most interestingly active in the ways the sound of a piece and its content interconnect or interfere with one another, which will happen, in the always-changing conditions of performance and listening—unpredictably.

Before concluding, I would like to mention two more ideas, which I think are important but not exclusively so.

Both these ideas have to do with renunciation or restriction, a kind of ascetic minimalism (it's a nice paradox that much of the music labeled minimalist, say, the earlier Philip Glass and Steve Reich, was basically good time music). One is the notion of musical poverty, of an avoidance of rhetoric, of the presence of silence or spaciousness, of sparseness of the irreducibility of material. One might think of music of Satie, Webern, Feldman, Lucier, Cage, for examples. The other notion is of what Adorno refers to as "the ideal of darkness," which does not simply match what he feels to be the darkness of the times, of social reality, but "does no more and no less than postulate that art properly understood finds happiness in nothing except its ability to stand its ground. This happiness," he continues, "illuminates the sensuous phenomenon from the inside. . . . blackness [darkness]—the antithesis of the fraudulent sensuality of culture's façade—has a sensual appeal." These notions, of poverty and darkness, would function, so to speak, to keep us honest; and Adorno adds the point that in that very function their music achieves its particular beauty. As I said, I find these ideas of critical importance but not exclusively so: necessary but not sufficient conditions for our work.

So what is our work? It is, I still believe, experimental music.

3

ROBERT ASHLEY

April 7, 1992

ALVIN LUCIER

I've known Bob Ashley since the early 1960s. I first met him in New York. He had driven from Ann Arbor to attend a concert in Town Hall in which I participated. At that time, I was director of the Brandeis Chamber Chorus devoted to the performance of contemporary music. We had been invited to perform a couple of works of Morton Feldman and Earle Brown in Town Hall. A couple of carloads of people drove down from Ann Arbor, Michigan, to hear that concert. Ashley had founded, with Gordon Mumma, one of the first independent electronic studios in the United States. It was a place that anyone could come and work. This was before studios really started to proliferate in all the universities in the country. At the same time,

Bob was the director of the Once Group, a group of musicians, visual artists, and architects in Ann Arbor that, along with Anna Halprin in California, created the first intermedia works. Under Bob's leadership, the Once Group created the most amazing performances in such unlikely places as parking structures, automobiles, trucks, hearses, and other alternative venues. He wrote numerous works for conventional instruments as well. I guess you could say that he was one of the first inventors of graphic notation, too. After his talk, I. M. Harjito and Sumarsam (rebabs), Subramanian (South Indian violin), and Roy Wiseman (double bass) will present a performance of one of his graphic scores, *In Memoriam: Esteban Gomez (Quartet).*

The most astonishing thing about Bob's work is his discovery that human speech is music. Once, as accompaniment to a Merce Cunningham dance performance in New York, Bob gathered some of his old Ann Arbor friends for an unrehearsed conversation. All they did was talk. That's all it was. It was compelling. It was music.

She Was a Visitor is a work for speaking chorus in which all the phonemes contained in the title sentence are detached and sustained for long breaths, revealing hidden meanings and images: "sh" (hush); "oo" (delight); "ah" (surprise); '"er" (hesitation), and so forth.

Wolfman was the loudest musical work one ever heard at that time. It was also the most ironic. Contrary to popular belief, the performer makes extremely soft vocal sounds. The loudness is produced by enormous amplifier gain, the feedback stopped only by the barely audible input from the vocalist.

Ashley does astonishing things with time in *String Quartet Describing the Motions of Large Real Bodies*. First he asks the players to bow slackened strings so slowly (one bow length up to ten minutes) and with such pressure that no continuous sound is produced, only pops and clicks. He then routes these signals through a series of delays of from five to 250 milliseconds (slow for computers, fast for humans), causing subtle shifts in timbre. These extremes of scale give the listener the uncanny feeling of slow and fast at the same time, as when a Boeing 747 barely moves, hovering, while landing.

For the last fifteen years, Ashley has devoted himself to creating a new genre of work: opera for television. I don't mean opera simply put on television, but opera for the medium itself. These wonderful pieces exist on video and can also be performed live. I am delighted that he is here to talk you in person.

ROBERT ASHLEY

I said I would talk about technique, and it's hard to start because Alvin stole some of my lines. Against all the wisdom of watching television, it occurred to me that because I was interested in music and words—without knowing anything more about it than that, and because I was working with people who were, lucky for me, great with words, I mean great, great talkers and willing and not afraid to do things with their voices—I got caught up with the idea of narrative music. All of you will have this experience. I went through a period of about ten or twelve years where everything was quite wonderful for me, working in concert not stage; then suddenly for political reasons everything was not quite wonderful, and I didn't do anything for four or five years. It occurred to me that, because of my peculiar obsession with words, television was the place that I should try to get into.

So I started working with the idea that I would make music for television. So far, not very much of it has been seen on television, not in the United States at least. But I have nothing to complain about. I started making pieces in which speaking was a form of music, and I got great composer-performers who were also great speakers to participate in my pieces. Then one thing led to another, and I found myself able to work on this idea that had been somewhat of an obsession with me—to just let the words be the music. That's pretty much what I've been working on for the past ten or twelve years.

I'm about at the end of it now. I have written forty half hours for television. It is like a series. When and if I finish producing them, I will retire. That's enough work to do in one person's lifetime. Probably it will take the rest of my life just to get them produced. So far, I have only eight of them produced, so I have thirty-two more of them to go. I have performed a lot of them in concert, however.

Basically, I take the smallest core ensemble for a particular opera, that is to say, the people who sing all the principal characters and the people who add to whatever music we bring with us. In that way, the singers are able to develop the characters, and I'm able to see what each piece needs, how it needs to grow. This is an introduction to an anecdote about technique. Right now I'm working on the last four so-called operas of this set. Each one is in an eighty-eight-minute format. Four parts of twenty-two minutes each, direct sequels to a piece I produced about twelve years ago that some of you might have seen parts of, called *Perfect Lives*. I produced that for British television. Typically, it hasn't been broadcast in the United States.

One of the ideas of the last four futuristic pieces is to make a map of our mental history as Americans, where we came from and where we're going. Naturally, we start in the ancient past and go into the future. Since I'm working on the last four right now, I've been dealing with the idea of how you show and dramatize a cultural technique. The gamelan ensemble you see behind me is obviously a dramatic version of a cultural technique, and we all presume that that technique can be articulated; that one person can tell another person how to do it brings with it the cultural technique. In other words, if you know how to do it and tell me how to do it, by virtue of me learning how to do it, I become part of it.

What we know about what we think are our roots in European music is almost exclusively embodied in techniques. Even though we are in Middletown, Connecticut, which is quite close to the Atlantic coast, for all sorts of bizarre reasons we pretty much have forgotten what our belief roots are. We haven't forgotten as much as if we lived in California. We operate with respect to European techniques pretty much the same way we operate with respect to the gamelan. We take a young person from Omaha, and we teach that young person to play Chopin. How bizarre. And what Alvin and I went through—especially what people of my generation went through—was that the notion of music composition became exclusively a matter of the organization of techniques. You've probably heard of Arnold Schoenberg. He had a technique. And you've probably heard of other people in the Viennese school who had techniques, something that you measure out and that you can talk about and learn how to do if you paid enough attention to it. In other words, you could learn Webern exactly the same way as you could learn the Macintosh. You would actually feel as if you were Webern.

After all, what is music about? You want to go back to that wonderful time when things were less complicated than they are now. Everybody would want to be Webern, and everybody would want to study Webern. So what Alvin and I went through—and a lot of other people—was that we were exposed to the notion of technique. At the same time, we heard—this is like a history—we heard rumors of American techniques. Chauvinistic considerations apart, it was an idea that there were different techniques. Instead of wanting to be Viennese, you would want to be whatever the other thing was. You would want to be Californian or you would want to be something else.

Throughout my life, I have been surrounded by techniques, all of which have almost no cultural value except as they appeared as packaged. If I adapted myself to the package, then presumably I could be . . . Charles Ives. There's a technique. It's a hundred years old. I mean, who's interested in Charles Ives? Nobody is interested in Charles Ives because it's too old. But, we all know about all of the techniques.

Having gotten to a certain age, I realized it was about time for me to produce a technique. I'm almost ready to go away, and I don't even have a technique to my credit yet. The other day, I had to give a lecture at a critic's conference. I asked for a show of hands. "Raise your hand if you've done a profound analysis of Morton Feldman, if you have taken a Morton Feldman piece to a place where you know where every note comes from." No hands. "How about Alvin Lucier?" No hands. "John Cage?" One guy's hand went halfway up. He had probably read *Silence*. "Phil Glass?" No hands. "Maggi Payne?" No hands. I asked, "How could one be a critic if you don't know facts?" Then I realized afterward that this was unfair of me because I was actually talking about techniques.

I've been trying to figure out what my technique is. This is a serious problem for me. It may not be a serious problem for you. We may be entering a cultural era where there are no techniques. Maybe we are all out of fashion, that there is some other thing going on. It may be that something is replacing technique. I don't know about this.

Now, to go back to the story of the opera. Just a couple of days ago, I was in New Mexico. I decided that I would make a collaboration between my idea and the ideas of a large community of Spanish Americans who modify cars. They call themselves low-riders. They take old American cars and transform them. They don't make them go faster. They don't make them go slower. They don't actually do much to the cars that could be considered different from the cars as they come from the factories in

Detroit. Probably some of you know about these cars. One thing they do is to put a hydraulic system on the four wheels, either independently or in pairs so that they can make the car jump up and down. They can actually make the car jump off the ground or they can make the car go right to the ground and just drive along scraping the ground. Or, they can make the front wheels go down and then drive sideways, scraping the front wheel. They do things with the mufflers like most American kids have done since the beginning of cars, because they make beautiful sounds. The engine is still connected to the transmission. The wheels turn and move. And they make the sound in the car louder than most American cars, but everything is superficial. The cars are extraordinary. When you are in the presence of one of them, you feel as if you're in the presence of a piece of art. Actually, it only occurred to me, finally, after I had been out there for a few times, that it was like being in the presence of quilts in the Amish country.

When you see one lowrider car, it's just a paint job. Or, if it jumps, it's just weird. And if a guy turns on the hi-fi very loud, you say, "That's just a hi-fi." It's odd in the same way that Watts Towers is odd, and all the other things that are our accumulations of American culture are odd. But when you see a hundred lowrider cars all in one parking lot, it's actually beyond my ability to speak of it. So I thought that I would ask these guys about their technique. I mean, how stupid could I be? I thought it would be clever and interesting if I could have them describe their technique, and I could put their descriptions in my piece, and then I could put that piece on television. That was my idea, among a bunch of other ideas. It was like I would ask a composer, "How do you write music?" And I would put that description of how you write music on television. How clever. Of course, none of them can describe their technique. I can actually talk more about their technique than they can. They would say, "Well, you know, me and my brother we just cut the springs in half and put it down and we put this . . ." And I would say, "When you cut the springs in half that makes it quite low, you know, and you don't have any shocks." He says, "Well, yah, you just take this piece of rubber out of a truck"—there's a piece of heavy-duty rubber that comes with a truck suspension—"and you put that underneath the bumper so that when the thing, like, hits the ground in a big bump it doesn't break the A-frame." Right? That's interesting, but he could say it in actually just half a sentence. He would just shrug and say, "You know . . . the rubber."

Then you ask, "Well, what about the paint job?" And he says, "Well, me and my brother, we just, like, do this, and then this, this, this." And what I had imagined would be a brilliant discussion of technique, you know, on the order of Schoenberg or some guy who wins the Nobel Prize—I'm in the presence of what I consider to be a rather extraordinary piece of art, and the guy can only just shrug his shoulders and say, "Well, that's what I do."

When I was enthralled by European technique, when I was reading Stockhausen, Boulez, Nono—brilliant composers whose music I loved—when I read their descriptions of their techniques, I was embarrassed because I didn't have a technique, and nobody I knew had any techniques. I always thought that I had the idea that American music was—American music meaning me and Alvin, but, yes, I mean Leonard Bernstein too—I had always thought that American music was primitive in the sense that the composer had a very limited historical perspective and an enormous command of detail by virtue of cultural isolation.

That's what primitivism is. If you cut any human being away from their society so that they have no externals—nobody telling them anything—then their obsession with the symbolic materials that they live with everyday, whether it's a quilt or cooking or music or, you know, whatever . . . Watts Towers becomes an example of a huge mastery of detail without reference to the outside world. This has been the story of American music. We see it in Charles Ives. We see it in Harry Partch. We see a beautiful remnant of it in John Cage. You probably see it in Alvin. You see it in me. You see it in all of my friends.

It's like Eskimo baseball. We see the example of people who have an idea of something that exists outside them. But, they didn't have any contact with the idea so they just started making it out of what they had around them. I thought that was characteristic of our music and that I was, how should we say, deprived or that it was sad that I was outside the historical mainstream. I thought the historical mainstream went from Vienna to Paris and that, since I was in either Michigan or California, it was a long way from the historical mainstream and that the mainstream would just go on as it always goes on. And I would just still be out there, and everybody would still be out there with me.

Having talked to the lowriders, I think I might have been wrong. I think I might have just changed my mind this weekend. I think I might have had a huge cultural conversion, which I would like to explain to you. I think that, in having said what I just said, then, I can just offer a few opinions. I think there is actually no cultural mainstream.

Maybe it's because of television. Maybe there was never a mainstream. Maybe we made it up. Maybe the whole idea of the mainstream is just an illusion. We have every reason to see that, for instance, Beethoven, to take a good example of a mainstream composer, comes at the intersection of wars, you know, Jesus, all that stuff! It's possible that he's just as primitive as I am. It's just that, for some other reason, he's interesting to us.

In my age group, I have been surrounded by, fascinated by, and obsessed by the actual facts of people living in North America who have no cultural contacts to what I consider to be mainstream. They have absolutely none, and they continue to make things. They will always continue to make things. I had just set them aside. You've probably all heard about Watts Towers. Every night this guy comes home and brings three tin cans, a pan, and a couple of pipes. He welds them together and makes a tower. Now that is not unusual. There was a time fifteen or twenty years ago when I was totally fascinated with this kind of American culture. I knew dozens of examples of people who made amazing sculpture, people who made amazing poetry, amazing music that nobody ever saw or heard. The only reason everybody saw Watts Tower is that Watts grew up around it. In the middle of Wisconsin—bang—a guy makes a totally amazing piece. I knew dozens of those examples and thought I was one of those examples. Maybe I am.

I have been trying to develop a technique that, in the context of European music, and in the context of American music, and in the context of Asian music, and in the context of everything is just totally my own. Idiosyncratic. Not my own because I want it. But it's not my own because I don't know anything else to do, and I'm not interested in anything else.

I've been trying to figure out how to make music that follows the rules of speech and that comes from all of the parent rules and conditions of speech. I start by speaking, instead of going into a room and playing the piano with some imagination of what that particular act is going to result in. Instead of imagining that it is going to be played by a great jazz ensemble or a great new music ensemble or a great orchestra, I go into the room and lock the door and talk to myself. And I keep on talking to myself until the music of the talk takes over. Until there are rules operating—for lack of a better word I call *musical* rules—until there are rules operating that govern the sounds that are coming out of my mouth. Tonight is not a good example. When that condition is satisfied, that's what I call composing.

As a result of having done that practice I know the tune, as it were. I know it backwards and forwards. I could write it down, or type it, or put it into a computer. I allow its manifestation on the page to be effectively a score. Now, that's not hard to understand for a composer. I mean, you can look at pretty much anything and analyze it visually, and you can use that as a metaphor for some sort of action.

And, as you all know, that metaphor can be more or less interesting depending on how seriously you take it. In the case of John Cage, the *I Ching,* or some other weird thing. The result can be grand or it can be not so grand depending on how seriously you're willing to go along with it, how deep you're going into it spiritually. So among composers, the question of using any particular manifestation, any particular form, is not a problem.

The obvious factor of what I see on the paper or on a computer screen or what I hear myself saying can be translated as any of the dimensions of music that we could name—pitch, duration, or any of the newer ones. I've been trying to allow this template, the notion of a plan, the notion of a three-dimensional or four-dimensional plan, a template that will give you back exactly what you put into it as in a machine template. I've been trying to get this so it will control the other aspects of the work, that is to say, the visual and the narrative aspects.

I found the notion of a technique at the beginning of these searches of mine fifteen years ago. I found the notion of a technique because I was coming from a relatively tame suburban Californian environment to New York City, but I wasn't staying long enough so that I could get immune to it. I was visiting New York a lot and, as a result, I was stunned and attracted by the number of people on the street who talk to themselves, who rant. I decided that I would try to learn how to do that. I know that there are a lot of prejudices against people who rant.

I recognized in myself a slight structural tendency to rant. I recognized that I had a very low level of Tourette's syndrome and that, either in addition to Tourette's syndrome, or as an embellishment to Tourette's, I had the tendency to repeat myself. I recognized that the tendency to say everything twice was actually the beginning of ranting. So I thought that was a good place to start. New York is full of people who are Nobel Prize winners in ranting. They are the Olympic athletes of ranting. I've never seen anything like the excellence and the high quality of ranting that you see in New York. New York has some of the greatest talkers in the world.

So I decided I would learn to rant. I practiced the state of mind that allowed me to rant. I actually got to the point, because I'm such a good musician—because I'm so obsessed with this idea—where I could actually rant. I didn't show off, but I got to the point where I could actually do it. And after three or four years of very serious study, I decided I would test it for myself to see if I was actually doing what I thought I was doing. I had access to the studio at Mills College one summer. I set the thing up so that all I had to do was push one button, and it would record anything that went on in the room. It would record it at very low levels. I knew how to do this. I left it there for two days while I went home and got in the mood to rant. Finally one evening, it seemed to be time. I went into the studio and I punched the button and I ranted. I actually allowed myself to make music.

The problem with why you can't play the piano is because, as you start playing, you get distracted by something outside you. Whatever that distraction is—in this case it could have been the distraction of a schedule; I could have worried about whether the tape was running out. I ranted for exactly forty-four minutes. Then I played it back and, indeed, it sounded just like what I thought it was supposed to sound like. I played it for my friends, and they were embarrassed for me. I was embarrassed for myself because I had actually practiced.

One time I was on an escalator in the San Francisco airport and right ahead of me there was a Chinese family—a man, his wife, and three or four kids. I just couldn't resist ranting. When they heard me, they actually ran. So I knew that I had something going. I knew that I could do it.

The trick is that what I had always imagined was happening in other people's ranting— happening in the way that you can see the larger scale of things by just looking at a little detail— when I had heard these people ranting, I knew that there was something going on that you could analyze just like technique. I decided that I would use this particular tape in combination with some other structure that I won't even bother to tell you about now but that was sort of electronic ranting. I decided that I would use this to illustrate a performance on videotape. In other words, I wanted to try it out in the world. I had somebody transcribe it for me who didn't know anything about the idea. I just said, "Please write it out. Write all the parts of the words, all the dot-dot-dots. Write everything you hear because I'm going to give it to a friend of mine to translate into French." When I got the transcription back, it was more organized than Webern. I'm not kidding you. It was more organized than Webern.

There were four themes. There were four incantations that were repeated. One of them was "You guys are all . . ."; I had noticed it when I would be at a party, when I was feeling the old Tourette's syndrome. I would go into the bathroom and say, "You guys are all, you guys are all . . ." for a few minutes, and then I would go back out to the party. Classic Tourette's syndrome. "You guys are all . . ." I've forgotten what the other three are. Each of them had four syllables. The forty-four minutes was in four parts. It was a suite. Maybe it was a sonata. I don't know. It was in four movements.

Now you understand that I was not doing this. You have to believe me that I was only ranting. You have to believe me. The four movements could be organized, could be analyzed around a module unit. I've forgotten what that unit was now. It was something like four minutes and twelve seconds or something like that. Each of the four movements had a theme that was repeated incessantly, which was made up of four syllables. Each of those four syllables, each of those four syllable themes, had a different accent pattern. “You guys are all . . .” is one. That’s like ba-dum ba-dum. Each had a different rhythm pattern. Each of the four had a subsidiary theme, which was made up of two, four, or eight syllables and a bunch of other things. It was as organized as Webern, I am telling you.

I knew I was onto something. So I’ve composed music like that ever since. That’s the way I do everything. I rant. I ranted *Perfect Lives*. *Perfect Lives* consists of seven half-hour episodes. Two of them I wrote in one sitting. I ranted them for a few days, a few weeks. Chu-ka, chu-ka, chu-ka, chu-ka, chu-ka, chu-ka, chu. Out it comes. A few of the other ones I did in two or three separate parts. If I had the time, I could go in and rant. I could actually write a big piece. I could actually say a big piece in the same way that a great jazz pianist could improvise a piece. So let’s quit.

4

MARYANNE AMACHER

November 7, 1995

ALVIN LUCIER

Neely Bruce reminded me that it was 1980 in Minnesota at the New Music America Festival where Maryanne Amacher inhabited the Victorian house of Dennis Russell Davis. The house was filled with the most extraordinary sounds one had ever heard. One of the characteristics of these sounds was that they were extremely loud, at least we thought they were loud then. I remember too that Maryanne had installed a series of petri dishes that had some sort of agar or culture in them. Nobody knew exactly why they were there. Was it simply the image of growing biological material? David Tudor once said that, sooner or later, we would be able to grow our own electronic equipment, you wouldn't need to manufacture it. A composer could use biological engineering techniques to grow his or her own amplifiers, for example. I think Maryanne had that image somewhere in mind as a possibility. It was that far out, futuristic.

I remember everyone standing outside the house that was bursting and exploding with sound. If you were brave enough, you'd go inside. It was like a steam room in a sauna; you would see how long you could stay in. People would say, "I was in for ten minutes." Another would counter with, "Well, I was in there for fifteen." Some people claimed they were in there the whole time, but I don't believe it. Stories went around that the police came and closed it, but I don't think that's true. For the past several years, John Cage has asked Maryanne Amacher to supply him with sound environments for various pieces. You'd go to a performance of Cage's *Lecture on the Weather*, for example, and hear the most miraculous and magical mixing of sounds. Somehow, with her, the sum of the mixing is much greater than the parts that go into it. A third thing occurs that is in a realm that is hard to articulate and understand. And that's one of the reasons why I've invited Maryanne Amacher here tonight, to see whether she might articulate in some way her wonderful, magical work.

MARYANNE AMACHER

Thank you very much. I should tell a story about Alvin. Alvin is one of the few people who has been intimately involved with the experiential aspects of music, rather than notes without ears. His experimental work is about how we perceive things, and how we hear them is very important now. But first, to get to my story. I remember at the Lincoln Arts Center, the Performing Arts Center Library, I heard this wonderful piece of Alvin's where he was going around the room along the walls—it must have taken about forty-five minutes. And for some reason, through the years, I thought it was some manifestation of his brain wave piece. But tonight he described to me that it was vibration amplification, bringing sounds in from outside. It was really an exciting experience for me at that time, just when I was studying music, to be able to witness this kind of activity going on. So I appreciate very much being here, and, as I said, in terms of the direction of our work with perception, I feel you are very fortunate to have such a man here to be able to study with him.

We have grown up in a time when we can actually discover so much more about how we hear, which of course in earlier music you could not do. When I began, I had tape recorders and loudspeakers, and I could observe how sound affected me not out of an interest simply to write notes but to discover aspects of it. We have always been able to do that, even in the analog world. Now, with much finer sophistication, there is so much to be discovered. Is the sound close or far away? Is it hitting your elbow, vibrating your whole body? Is it something you seem to see? All these things are really perceptual modes, or what really captures the experience and how you create it. You don't create it with notes or sounds; you create it when you're making immersive worlds and constructing these aspects of our perception. Recently, there was a symposium at Mills College on John Cage. There were many theorists involved and it lasted for four days, and a good bit of it dealt with wanting people to talk about his influence in different areas—writing, art, music. It was very important for him to have been at Wesleyan when he wrote his book, *Silence*. He was twenty-five years old in 1937 when he wrote his *Credo* on music and described how, more and more in the future, people would be dealing with noise. He asked incredible questions. He was always paying attention to what was going on. In 1937, Cage wrote about defining parameters of sound electronically in the future. In 1942, he quoted two acousticians about the different kinds of electronic instruments that might be possible. He was aware of what was happening in terms of acoustics and sound at that time, as well as just writing his music and being happy with that. The environment that he came out of must have been incredible. He was born in 1912. Women were still wearing long skirts. Suddenly, he's in this world of music where conservatory students are practicing Beethoven and Mozart, and here this man comes up with a million questions. He was thinking about how to develop this music twenty-five years from then. It's practically sixty years since he wrote that. Just last week I read a review of Sonic Youth, and the big headline was: "It's the Noises That They Want." Normally, with similar groups, it's the first chords they relate to, but here, with Sonic Youth, it's the noise that they and their fans relate to. John, at that time, was fascinated by sound effects. Radio stations had all kinds of sound effects used to make the early radio shows. He described how, with all of these sounds, we would have the whole world at our disposal. We now have this in sampling. He was a liberator in the sense of freeing people's minds from this whole music thing, which was patriarchal and habituating. If we could do cybernetic simulation of John's kind of thinking right now and imagine ourselves projected fifty years from now . . . It's not so different. We're in such an extraordinary time with developments in technology. It wasn't that different in his time when all of these things were just about to begin. Now they're about to turn over in an incredible way again. He wrote about composers no longer having to deal only with musical notes on a page and the reality of having the whole world of sound and/or noises. We now have that. There are many questions now in the area of memory. In ten years, things will have become so small, and the memory in computers will be so large that there will be tremendous implications on how we think about time and form in music. There is an optical form of memory. Physical objects the size of a quarter could contain eight days of music. There are forms using quantum logic for memory that would increase by a hundred-fold what we have now. Also, we can think of creating characters that might exist for five minutes now and for ten hours two weeks from now. This is where time comes in. You could actually create sound for five minutes; then there wouldn't be anything for two hours—people would have this in their house—and suddenly something would come in like some strange act, coming from out of somewhere. All the limitations we've been under for doing these kinds of pieces with time are really something to think about.

What we have explored very little as musicians are sounds that our ears create. There is good research about this. Your ears emit sound a few minutes after you die. They actually emit as well as absorb and receive sound. In the early days, musicians probably were aware of this phenomenon more intuitively. In Tibet, people tune and produce sounds that their ears create. Some of these sounds are called difference tones, which are second-order effects that are mechanical responses of the ear—actually the signal going through your ears—then being put together in some part of your brain as an information pattern that actually gives shape and form. These are very powerful. You've probably heard it in your own music with certain kinds of beat phenomena—not amplitude modulation. It is an effect that comes from the unison when you have stereo, you have to have two ears, with the major third or fifth you can actually have it in mono. It's not beating. No one knows what's creating it. It's part of your nervous system that's putting this information together. It happens in a lot of ways in my music [that] I'm not even aware of. I'll go back and try to hear something, and if I've been listening too long to one part so that I'm already kind of programmed in my head, I really have to be careful because you're shaping a lot of melodies from basic information. I was drawn to it recently by some CD collections that I'm on. I'm not very interested in ordinary CDs. I would like to make interactive audio CDs. People would have scores in their home and could do various transformations. My own work is done architecturally. I use multispeaker systems in several rooms, so it's not very fitting to have two speakers in your living room. I was startled to hear the other music because the composers used a lot of what's almost like exoskeletons to me. They put in not so much reverb but delays. It makes such a solid chunk of something that it's like your mind . . . it's like you're not reading that much in anymore. They don't sound that unique because they have a very strong color. There are many aspects to it, to reading in, which our minds do. The strong effects when our ears produce other tones actually sound like they are right here. You feel you can actually touch them. In the past, it was not possible to study difference tones. People used to hear them intuitively, but now you can actually make programs to control them. You do not have to think only of the tones in the room. You can also give equal notion to the sounds the listener creates in his ears. The sound the listener creates in his ears is as much a sonic dimension as the acoustic tones that are sounding in the room. You can create them consciously. When you studied harmony in school, you learned about musical tones. Actually, the tones that your ears produce are responsible for why you recognize a major third or fifth. At Johns Hopkins, they call it otoacoustic emission. They have interesting articles in which they call it "a tiny loudspeaker within the ear." This is very much in the commercial world of music. At Universal Studios, in the *Back to the Future* exhibit, one of the effects they use is a very low subliminal tone, maybe twenty cycles per second. They even have a name for it—frequency injection—and it's used to make a much more thrilling ride. I read a book called *A Textbook of Aviation Physiology* that gave different vibration frequencies for different parts of the body. I was shocked to discover that in very low regions, the effects are critical. At six cycles per second you might feel sick, but at eight you might feel good. At seven it affects your eyes or may even cause blindness. People working in theme parks are paying attention to this phenomenon, whereas people in the musical world are not.

As someone who does location-based installations and performances, I go to a place and, if it's a major work, I usually work there for three weeks—once I got to work six weeks—with the sound because I want to make something happen. To that end, I have developed what I call *Mini Sound Series* in which I invent sound characters. Maybe one part of the work is one week long, then it continues into the next week or the week after. It's wonderful when people come back.

The first installation I did was in San Francisco. I had six weeks to work on it. Mostly I do them in Europe or Japan because most people are reluctant or don't understand that to create sound for certain specifications, you need to work and be there at the location. I recently read about people working for two months on location-based installations in Las Vegas—working out and perfecting everything on hard discs. Once they get it running, they do trials with numbers of people; they can alter things on the hard disk; it's an accepted thing. Whereas in the field of alternative music, if you want a little time, they think, "My goodness, give over the space to a composer for this long?" I think things will change now. Another tendency is the creation of interactive scores for people at home. CD-ROMS are very primitive, and probably audio would actually be more effective. The visual aspect is not going to take off until we have real three-dimensional experiences we can get by wearing glasses or in some other way. We actually had this in the home instead of CD-ROM where you're looking at a screen. But, actually, there are many ways of thinking about designing incredible worlds and scripts in which people may make transformations of your music and bring other things in.

Right now, I am doing two interesting projects. One is called *Gong*. People are studying the titanic oscillations of the sun.

They're extremely low; each cycle takes about five minutes. There are six listening posts around the world that are tracking these slow waveform patterns. The research will tell us about the origins of the universe. There is another one that sends sounds into the ocean in order to study global warming. The waves start from California and travel around the world under water. You know that sound travels faster in warmer temperatures; therefore it's a good way to study this. But they've had to delay the project because people complained that it would be very damaging to the animals. But they did something worse. They have now decided that they will send sounds only two days a week. The poor whales get a rest and then, *whammo*, they turn it on again. You could call up any of those laboratories. You could design a whole script that people could have at home with some music you make. You can bring in the ocean; you can bring in the waveforms from the sun. It's incredible the kind of worlds you can invent now. When you go back in time, you realize the only way to have a first-person experience was when, for example, you experienced a symphony orchestra. You didn't hear music anywhere else. You went to the symphony and entered this magical place. The tendency to get more and more personalized worlds developed when records appeared, and you could experience music in your own living room. You could get into any world you wanted. We are entering an age of customization—genes, drugs, you name it—everything is being customized. As a composer, you could even think of having people's readouts for customizing music for certain bodily rhythms and parts. It's not that far-fetched. We are in a time when we can make scores and give people opportunities to customize worlds that we initiate as composers, creators, or writers; then people may develop them in their homes. One only has to imagine these things. This is where thinking about different kinds of new forms and time is very exciting. I don't think in the future there will be such a split between forms of pop music and alternative music. Already they are coming together. If art music continues, maybe the only distinction will be that people doing art music might design worlds that somehow are more specialized or exotic or even have watermarks, because music no longer will be made for millions. We've just gone through a weird period in which creepy avant-garde composers were composing weird music. Maybe they're emblems for what in thirty years will be the watermark as a composer. You might make it for one or two people, or one museum, where it would be theirs in this perfect way. It doesn't have to get played in a million restaurants and bookstores, like poor Bach or Mozart. But you would have a watermark, a signature, and an electronic signature that someone would have a key to. And that's it. Many options are open. It's just a matter of raising the questions about them.

I just read an interview with Nicholas Negroponte, the director of the MIT Media Lab, who just published a book, *Being Digital*. The interviewer asked him what he thought about biotechnology, and he said, "Well, it probably is going to be the twenty-first century, but no one knows." Even to talk about machines doesn't make a lot of sense now. It's really more the physics of these elements and the potential and being aware that, for example, if there is a biological memory it will be capable of storing much more. If things develop in that direction, how are you going to function as a composer? Are you going to sit in a room and write scores and play your keyboard? You might instead be designing auditory enhancers. You might rather make a piece about the sun. Maybe you'll discover a way to enhance your sensitivity such that you actually could experience those low sounds. I don't know if that's possible. You could design that piece Alvin was talking about. It was called *Living Sound: Patent Pending*.

In 1980, they passed a law for patenting life forms. I had read about that four months before I made *Living Sound*, in the same weekend the law was passed. It was exciting to me that it was a synchronous event. It took place in Dennis Russell Davies's music room. I had petri dishes and a funny text on music stands about making violins. There were odd visual things around the house. A biochemist had given me some petri dishes with a growing medium of agar. I had a text about the atoms in your body, having been there all these years. In the sunroom, I had an audiocassette recording of when the radio telescope designed to send signals into deep space was inaugurated. The director of the program gave a little speech about how we were the greatest and most powerful country in the world and were sending the first messages off to a planet or star or wherever it was going. He said, "We are standing in the most powerful spot in the world." Then he said, "More details will be available at lunch." Everyone applauded, as if they were at a concert. It was silly. This incredible thing was going on. They were sending signals billions of light years away and he said such stupid things. We hadn't even made it to breakfast.

When I was a music student, what I really loved about the piano was to listen to all the stuff that came out in the overtones. I really wanted to learn about that, so I studied it myself.

It's the same thing, playing these things over and over again in the same forms, and it's all so much out of habit and it's fine, but there's a whole lot more you can imagine. There's a lot of room for it because people will want to create these worlds at home. You can create different atmospheres, worlds where people can enter the sun, for example. It's endless. It's a very exciting time because we can hear everything, and, of course, we can create visual worlds to go along with this as well. I recently read about bridges and walls that sing, and there are just so many ways, I mean, I think the whole other area to think about are modes, are ways of presenting music. That's a whole area to think about because there are other ways of doing it than putting on pieces at a concert. It would be wonderful if there were buildings designed for sound, like there are art museums. Maybe there will be because people will be able to do a lot at home, make a lot of different musical experiences; but they obviously can't, I mean, not everyone, unless you're Bill Gates and have this incredible house, you can't really have a kind of experience that you could in a place that was dedicated to sound with multiple loudspeakers and sound that moves around. That will probably happen. I see signs of that. Often, I look at what's happening in other parts of the world. For example, Disney has bought several buildings in Times Square. They're investing in the future because they know people are going to want to go out and have a certain kind of entertainment besides just being in their homes. It was an odd time for them to invest in that because there is so much investment in media right now—interactive television and all that. They want to take over these theaters—it is kind of curious.

I am very struck by the game *Myst*. You're probably familiar with the CD-ROM game *Myst*. Two years ago, they would have had some silly melodies in that actual scene. It's this kind of sound that perceptually you have to read in. When I was listening for a while, I actually became hypnotized by it. It reminded me a lot of my first works in which I installed microphones in different remote locations. They were called city links, and a microphone could be by the ocean in one city and then another in another city; then I would bring these remote locations together in mixing. Sometimes in these ocean experiences, particularly at night, it wasn't the waves but just the air, and it would be very quiet. It was fascinating, you couldn't tell quite what was in the air. This was the kind of phenomenon that was on *Myst*. Two or three years ago, they would have used a funny little tune instead of this partially colored noise. You actually have to read in and construct your own meaning, however unconsciously. People relate to them perhaps because they're familiar, but it's a different kind of involvement. I don't think this game would have been so popular a few years ago if it used music, as it is now.

Maybe I should say something about my work. When I did these remotes, I was at MIT. I picked up signals with a microphone in Boston Harbor, coming into my studio on a high-quality telephone line. It was great because if I went somewhere, I could make another link to it and install it either in a gallery, or do a performance or whatever I wanted with it. I actually lived with it for three to four years. Initially, I did it not because I wanted the sounds of birds or seagulls or other environmental sounds. I really wanted to learn about the spatial aspects. So I carefully installed the microphones where I could hear sounds far away or close by. I absorbed the space unconsciously. I would come home late at night and turn the system on instead of turning on the radio or a record, and because of the transmission, I had a more detached perceptual space. After a certain period of time, I realized there was a constant tone. That got me interested in thinking about the subliminal tones that are around us. I created a series called *Tone of Place.* In Boston, when I measured, it was ninety-three cycles per second. Later, I put a microphone in Battery Park in New York. It made me think about where you grow up and the kind of tone you unconsciously hear. What does it mean? I never followed it through, but it was an interesting thing to think about. I made quite a number of those pieces and transmissions, some from here to Europe. After that, I developed the architectural aspect of my music. It actually came with thinking about the advances in software, that if I was creating something, I wanted to create something that would not be so easily made a variation of or replicated via software. I took that as a challenge. I wanted to make something that was more dramatic. I discovered that if I installed the sound with multiloudspeaker systems, [I] might make very interesting shapes or patterns, but if I install it architecturally, I might be able to get the sound to travel around behind that back wall to meet another sound. I could actually work with the physical properties of the room or the building itself. Acousticians call that structure-borne, verses airborne, sound. The wavelength for airborne middle C is four feet, whereas in structure-borne sound it's twenty-two feet. Maybe that's why quiet sounds, when I have them installed structurally, have a clear, magical presence. They don't sound as if they're coming out of loudspeakers and hurting your ears. It became very exciting for me to do works that involved more than one room. I've had some good opportunities to do that recently in Japan, where there was a main space and four other adjacent areas. In one of these areas, there was a curved stone structure that had a different acoustic from the main space. I'm not in the other rooms, so I can't hear it. So I have to know everything, I have to work there, and I have to learn the acoustics of the place for a period of time so that I know what I'm producing because it's very controlled. So I know that if I want to make an analogy between that back room and here, or I want to make a certain kind of tone fusion . . . so I'll know if someone's in here, what it feels like and what is out there. And you can make many different possibilities—I might have a zone of power, like this curved sound space. It was amazing. When I first went there to see the space, we were walking out on a curve and I said, "We have to have sound here," because it went up a hill! It was curved like in an old castle even though it was a new building, and the engineer said, "We can put a speaker there." And I said, "Maybe we don't need to." And we didn't. I was able to get the sound from the speaker in the preceding room. The sound seemed to be hanging in the air. As you walked through, it kept getting louder and louder; of course there wasn't any speaker there. It was like a hologram.

This past year I did one in a Kunsthalle in Austria. It was an old, large monastery. There were seven rooms; a big main space with a high altar, five rooms in the back, and a crypt down in the basement. You went down these stone steps. I chose different kinds of music for that, whereas in Japan I could make very distinct things as if something was up here, or here, or you heard back there, or something coming from very far away, whereas in the other place everything . . . it was just floating. I couldn't use any pulse music. I love those characteristics. In my *Mini-Sound Series*, I like to work with narrative involvements. It's interesting, the communication with an audience and their reactions. I've done about eight of them. The audiences are exciting, particularly the ones that are extended over five or six weeks. It's such a different experience to go somewhere and do an overnight piece. I guess when you're as experienced as I am, you like getting in there. It's proved to me to be a good way to do it. Thank you.

ALVIN LUCIER

We'll just have to ask you back.

5

LA MONTE YOUNG

November 5, 1996

ALVIN LUCIER

You are lucky if you come into contact with a single germinal artist in your lifetime whose work you know well and whom you know in a personal manner. I have been lucky to know two already in my lifetime: one is John Cage, whom we're all very well acquainted with here at Wesleyan; the other is La Monte Young. I couldn't begin to list the first things he did, that hadn't been done before, that then would become part and parcel of everybody's music. That's what I mean by germinal—somebody gets an idea that proliferates and spreads out and can be used in productive ways by other artists.

La Monte Young was the first composer to explore music with long sound durations. Early in his life, he discovered a world of self-awareness and perceptiveness by paying attention to something for a long time. Since the art of music is concerned with time, it was a very provocative and innovative thing to do. It spurred a whole genre of new age and drone music. Along with that came thinking about the purity of intervals and how tuning and very close attention to pure intervals affects one who experiences them. The idea of a piece that could last a lifetime, if not several lifetimes, as well as paying attention to one sound for a very long time are just two of the things that La Monte envisioned that defined experimental music. One also has to mention the beautiful light sculptures that Marian Zazeela, Young's lifelong partner, exhibits simultaneously with La Monte's performances and installations. During a recent performance of his one-and-a-half-hour long work for string quartet, *Chronos Kristalla*, at BAM Marian said that she "sequenced slowly dissolving colors on the poetically configured back wall of the stage while alternating complementary and contrasting colors on the musicians." The lights changed so slowly that one only noticed the changes after they had occurred.

I feel very fortunate to have been able to teach La Monte's work from the very beginning of my tenure here at Wesleyan in 1968. Every year in Music 109 we sing his *Composition 1960 #7*, letting students experience being in one musical interval for a long time. Tonight, eighty students from my Music 109 class will perform an hour-long version of his *Poem for Chairs, Tables, and Benches.* So, it is a wonderful honor for me to have this chance to invite somebody so essentially important to the world of music and art, and that is La Monte Young.

LA MONTE YOUNG

I prefer it if you [students] ask me questions because I want to find out what you're thinking about, what kind of interests you have, and, in the course of it, I will start talking about ideas that relate to what you're interested in.

QUESTION

I'd like to know about your abandonment of chance.

LA MONTE YOUNG

As most of you probably know, if you've read something about me, I became interested in chance when I was at Darmstadt. I was especially impressed when I met David Tudor. I thought he was the greatest living performer of contemporary music. He was a big inspiration for me. At the same time, I observed how much of himself he put into these works in spite of all the chance techniques involved. But it wasn't until around 1960 that I began to lose interest in chance. And one of the things I began to notice, if you know my *Trio for Strings*, which I composed in 1958 just after I got my BA at UCLA, was that although it was a serial work, it broke new ground: it was the first work composed entirely of long-sustained tones and silences. Additionally, each tone or each interval had its own point of entry and point of exit, and, in that sense, it was rather contrapuntal and harmonic at the same time. The intervals were very carefully selected and thought through, and I had begun to develop my own harmonic language, in that these chords, which I later called Dream Chords, began to emerge. A simple Dream Chord, for instance, consists of G—C—C-sharp—D. That's one position of a Dream Chord. The same chord, G—C—D—C-sharp is also a Dream Chord. There are inversions: G—D—C-sharp—C and G—D—C—D-flat. Almost all of the harmonies in the *Trio for Strings* are based on these chords. Harmonies like that had already begun to develop in *for Brass*, 1957, and in *for Guitar*, 1958.

But then, after *Trio for Strings*, I began to discover John Cage.

I went to Darmstadt in the summer of 1959, where I met David Tudor. Stockhausen talked a lot about John Cage in his advanced composition seminar. I came back very inspired with the kinds of sounds that David and John were beginning to work with, and I was also interested in the idea of chance. I composed *Vision*, which took thirteen minutes of time and used random numbers to determine the points of entry and exit of events. I predetermined the number of events and set of events and then used various techniques to determine which of these events would receive which durations and therefore find a way to fill up the thirteen minutes of time. I composed *Poem for Chairs, Tables, and Benches* in January 1960. This piece was entirely based on random techniques; you would even determine the duration of the piece randomly. It could be a year, a thousand years, a second, or no length at all. There were a lot of possibilities depending on what parameters you chose to work within.

But as time went on, and I began to work more and more with the kinds of long-sustained tones that I had been working with in *Trio for Strings* and in the middle section of *for Brass*, I began to think more and more about longer periods of time, extended duration relationships, and I began to observe that . . . well, really, it came about around the time I created the *Four Dreams of China*, which was in December 1962. I decided that each one of the Dream Chords that I described to you a few minutes ago could be the total harmonic material for one composition. And having decided that, I evolved a set of rules within the framework of which the performers would improvise. Since I had grown up on jazz, I was interested in improvisation. I was interested in having intervals and textures of the type that were in Trio for Strings. It was a completely notated work, every timbre, every dynamic marking. It lasted fifty-eight minutes. In Four Dreams of China, I set up harmonic rules. Let's take the case of the dream that goes G—C—D—C-sharp. The C-sharp was, in my mind, a very dissonant tone, and I developed a set of rules whereby the D, C, and G could play together in any kind of relationship. But the C-sharp could only play alone, or with the D, or with the D and the C, or with the D and the C and the G. The C-sharp could not play alone with the G, it could not play alone with the C, and it could not play with the C and G without the D. So the D always had to be in for the C-sharp to be there. The C-sharp could be alone, or it could play with the D; the D had to be in with the C-sharp, if the C was there. Then the C and the D had to be in with the C-sharp, if the G was there. These were the rules that the performers improvised with. Later on, in the '80s, I decided to make a Melodic Version of this original Harmonic Version in order to allow wind instruments to better play the piece and be able to have the full chord and sustain various intervals.

At the time—1962—I created the *Four Dreams of China*. In this first version, which we call the Harmonic Version as opposed to the Melodic Version that I created in the '80s, I began to conceive of the idea of a composition that could be without beginning and end. I had already touched on the idea in the rules for *Poem for Chairs, Tables, and Benches*. But in *Four Dreams of China* I decided that, in the same way that you can have rests during performances onstage, one can also think of the work in larger terms. And if you have the same set of pitches in two different performances, the two performances could be considered part of one performance with a long silence between them. In *Composition 1960 #7*, which I composed in July 1960—the B and F-sharp fifth piece—the instructions are "To be held for a long time." This was probably the beginning of the idea, the step between the concepts that might happen in *Poem* and deciding that it *was* happening in the *Four Dreams of China*. Once I had the idea that the silences between concerts were like big silences, even in daily rehearsals of the same piece, that the same piece was still going on and it was developing over time. Actually, it was the same piece. And when you work with improvisation with sets of rules, you have a sense of evolution from rehearsal to rehearsal to concert. It's never the same piece. It's the same framework, the same concept, same algorithm, but it doesn't sound exactly the way it sounded the last time or the next time you play it.

I began to observe that I was very interested in sounds that took place over long periods of time. It was difficult to do concerts the way I wanted. It became a waste of time to put silences into the pieces, no matter how randomly composed. The real problem that confronted me was how would I ever get a chance in my lifetime to make as much sound as I wanted to make. Once I discovered that that was the real problem—and most people won't pay my prices to do the concerts, most people won't give me the conditions that I want—there are these enormous periods of silence. Finally, somebody goes for it. So I fill that up with sound. The way that we do *Poem for Chairs, Tables, and Benches* now, as just a block of sound starting when it starts and ending when it ends, is exactly an example of this approach toward sound. The problem is that there isn't really enough sound. There aren't enough situations where you can really hear sound taking place over extended periods of time. What you usually get is a little variety show, a piece for ten minutes, one for twenty minutes, continuous sensory titillation. Concert producers want to please the crowds. I am really interested in getting into states that are much more meditative and profound and that utilize sound as a way to tune in to the structural relationships of the universe.

John Cage was a noble person, and as long as he had David [Tudor], he had the noblest performer of all time. He could write extraordinarily aloof chance works, hand them to David, and have a performance that was a masterpiece. Then, he would give it to an orchestra, and many times he actually admitted, you know, "I'm very discouraged about what they're doing, you know. They're doing this, they're doing that." They didn't really have these noble thoughts that John had in mind. They had their own thoughts; in fact, they thought it was silly. And what he got wasn't really what he wanted. Now, you can say he shouldn't want something. Why does he want something if he's writing these chance compositions? Well, turns out he actually had something in mind. And I found that, after working with chance for just a couple years, I thought it was fine for John. It really represented his approach to meditation. You know, he said to me, "We're opposite poles; we're like two sides of a coin." Positive can't exist without negative, and negative can't exist without positive, night and day. He was interested in a kind of meditation that grew out of a certain kind of Zen that accepted things as they were and let things flow. But I became very interested in a kind of meditation that was coming out of yoga and had to do with focus, concentration, discipline, and really knowing what you were going to do and making up your mind and being in control and deciding what you were going to do with your life.

And this relates directly to the kind of work that I do with tuning, for instance. John would let somebody make a bunch of noises. Fine. I'm very interested in noise. But I also know what kind of intervals I'm interested in and what kind I want to produce, and I became clearer and clearer about it as my life went on. I finally decided it was a total waste of time for me to work with chance and that I should be doing what I knew I should be doing and following my inspiration and listening to the chords I really like to listen to and determining the intervals I wanted to hear, setting up the structures that I wanted to take place, and trying to organize my life and my music the way I wanted it to be, and that's why I stopped. It was a great lesson, and I got a lot out of it. Next question.

QUESTION

Your piece, *X for Henry Flynt*, had a lot of repetition, and you described that you were trying to gain control. Is repetition actually control?

LA MONTE YOUNG

Repetition implies control. For something to be able to repeat exactly, it has to be totally in control. That piece is unique of all my works. But, clearly, it's very much related to everything else of mine; it's the only piece that uses repetition in this obvious way. There were much more subtle kinds of repetition, in my sopranino saxophone playing or in *The Well-Tuned Piano*. But, yes, I think that piece is all about control. Just as in the fifth piece, *Composition 1960 #7*, you try to make it exactly the same and perfect. Many variations take place by themselves over time. The same thing happens in *X for Henry Flynt*. The performer does his best to make every stroke of the gong exactly the same, and, of course, it's impossible. So the variation, depending on the capabilities of the performer, can be more or less subtle.

QUESTION

Tell me about an experience you've had in one of your *Dream Houses*.

LA MONTE YOUNG

When I go into my *Dream Houses*, I become involved in the complex of frequencies. How many of you have heard the current *Dream House* that I have in New York City right now? A few people have. This particular *Dream House* has, I think it's thirty-five discrete frequencies. And all of the frequencies . . . how many people know anything about my *Dream Houses* at all? Who's never heard of my *Dream Houses*? OK. Let me tell you what they are. Some time after I created the *Four Dreams of China,* but not long after, since I had conceived of pieces that would have no beginning and end and that would go on in time, I began thinking about, well, where could you really set up a piece and let it run? So, I conceived of this idea of the *Dream House*, where originally it was going to be just musicians, and it would be a building where the musicians could live as well. And they would have little monitor speakers in their own apartments so they could be listening to how the piece was developing in the main space. It would take about eighty musicians, I figured, to have a team of maybe eight playing all the time. The piece would run continuously. And this was the beginning concept of a *Dream House*. And I found after doing a few short-term *Dream Houses* with live musicians, and going to Europe with two tons of electronic equipment and six to eight people, that it would become very expensive to be able to pay musicians to keep it going continuously.

And gradually in the '60s, we began to move sufficiently into the age of electronics that more and more stable sine wave oscillators became available. By the '70s, we were easily getting them phase locked, and we went into digital by the late '70s. And, eventually, you had young people like David Rayna making the Rayna synthesizer, which you could program with a computer and enter ratios of intervals with rather large numerators and denominators and have them precisely in tune. Forget about the Korg's and Kurzweil's that have a resolution of 1200 cents to an octave. The Rayna synthesizer is—well, it's not perfect. Some people talk about it as if it were. How many of you know about acoustical beats? Beats are when you have two tones; let's say you have two pure sine waves. And when you get within a certain threshold, you begin to be able to observe beats. The threshold is usually described to be around a minor third. It becomes clearer when you get down to around 9/8 which is like D to C. You begin to notice, if the interval is harmonically related—that is, if the two frequencies can be represented as the numerator or denominator of some whole-number fraction—then the beating that you hear is periodic. If it's not representable by a whole-number fraction, then the beating is nonperiodic. And as you make the interval smaller, down toward a semitone, and gradually smaller than a semitone and closer and closer to unison, the amplitudes of the two sine wave frequencies add algebraically. And what this means is, you have something like [draws in air with finger], this is the way they usually portray a sine wave. That's one vibration of a sine wave, and there's a line going through the middle of that. And when the frequencies get very, very close, or fairly close together, the amplitudes add. So it means when you get two of the peaks lining up, the two add together and they get twice as high. And if you put the thing completely out of phase, 180 degrees, so that you have the peak of one where the valley of the other is, they completely cancel each other out, and you get silence. And so, if you have the frequency fairly close, the beats are going along like [sings], and the closer you get them together, the slower the beats become. So that if you have a bowed instrument, for instance, there's a threshold of possibility of how in tune you can get an interval. You can never get the interval more closely in tune than the duration of a beat that lasts the length of a bow change, because as soon as the bow changes, you introduce change. And this change is an interruption in the same way that the beat is a kind of interruption. So these are called acoustical beats, and they're the only way to tune an interval precisely.

You know, we differentiate between pitch and frequency. Pitch is your subjective sense of whether a tone is high or low, and frequency is the actual reality of that tone. So that with beats you can tune frequency very precisely. And with pitch it can be a rather complex situation. I've had very good musicians performing in my groups, and we perform with sine wave drones, and we tune to the drones and match our voices and instruments to them. And we found that if people just listened, using their best subjective ears, that a couple of people sitting in two different places would sing two completely different pitches. That's because pitch is subject to loudness. Loudness is to amplitude as pitch is to frequency. Loudness is how loud you think something is; amplitude is how loud it actually is. And we found that the same musicians could be using pitch to tune and not both sing the same pitch, because one could be sitting in the node of the sine wave and the other in the antinode.

How many of you know about standing waves? It's easiest to notice with a sine wave in an enclosed space. How many people know what a sine wave is? Good. A sine wave is the only waveform that has only one frequency component. It can be the building block of sound—you can't make it any simpler. Sine waves are very beautiful; they sound like a flute or a harmonic, but they have even less color, because they have no harmonics. So if you put a sine wave in an enclosed space, it will find places in the room that will organize it. It will be forced to organize itself according to the structure of the room in such a way that in some places it will be louder, and in some places it will be softer. And what happens when you go into one of my *Dream House* environments, for example, since it's created completely of sine waves, is you can walk in and out of the loud spots and the soft spots. And it becomes very complex if you have as many as thirty-five tones because the low frequencies have long wavelengths. You can walk maybe all the way across the room before you get from the loudest to the softest point, and the high frequencies can have tiny wavelengths so that you just barely move and you can move in and out of the nodes. So, if two musicians are sitting listening to a sine wave in an enclosed space and trying to tune to it, and they're tuning by pitch as opposed to by frequency, one of them will hear it louder, and the other one will hear it softer, and they'll both have a different impression of pitch. So you just cannot tune that way; you have to use beats. These acoustical beats are the way to tune and be precisely in tune, and this way you're in tune every time and it never fails. It's a very interesting study.

One of the things I'm interested in in relation to my *Dream Houses* is this concept of the drone state of mind. Some of you know that one of the reasons that Indian classical music evolved the most elaborate system of tuning, until we got into more modern times, is that it always took place over a drone. If you have a constant to which you can always return and refer to, it's like having a home, then you can develop very elaborate relationships because you always have this one fixed entity to come back to. When you go into a *Dream House*, the sine waves are there, and they're fixed in frequency; they don't change. You get different impressions of pitch and impressions of loudness and this sensation of being able to create your own melodies and harmonies as you walk in and out of the standing wave patterns. The standing wave patterns, then, are really a type of resonance. Simple resonance is when you have a frequency that starts at that wall, hits that wall, and gets back to that wall, just in time for the next positive pulse. You know, the way frequency is described as positive and negative pulses. Just think of a loudspeaker going positive, negative, positive, negative, positive, negative, producing a frequency. So a resonant frequency is a frequency that is just such that it starts at that wall, A; hits that wall, B; gets back to that first wall, A; just in time for the next positive pulse. So it's adding to what's already being produced. So that's simple resonance. But there are other kinds of resonance that take place in enclosed spaces. Some simple resonances and other angles and so forth. So standing wave patterns are these kinds of patterns that take place in enclosed spaces.

The concept of the drone state of mind is that each periodic pulse of the air molecule patterns hits the eardrum. For low and mid-range frequencies it's especially true that these pulses make it all the way through the synapses up to the cerebral cortex with pretty much a pulse pattern, so that the brain is receiving this pattern of pulses. This pattern of pulses can become like a reference pattern. In the same way that you already have patterns taking place in your body that you use as reference patterns, a set of frequencies in the sound environment can become a new set of reference patterns. In the same way that in Indian classical music they were able to develop this complex system of *srutis* because the pitches were always performed over a drone, in a *Dream House* as you spend time in it, you can establish a new foundational system based on this set of referential frequencies, which are actually, in the case of the current *Dream House*, using relationships that are based on very high prime number ratios.

Those of you who know about systems of musical languages know that in many systems you can reduce the system to a simple set of primes. Like in Western classical music, everything factors down to 2, 3, and 5. And in Indian classical music, I would say most of it really factors down to 2, 3, 5, and 7. Various Greek theorists did a little bit of work with higher primes, and over time people like Helmholtz became interested in more and more complex intervals, and we finally got ourselves into the twentieth century where you have composers like Harry Parch and Ben Johnson really starting to think about primes and getting a little bit into higher primes. But the question is how to find your model to listen to these primes. You have to be able to analyze your way up into the harmonic series. And this is where the Rayna synthesizer became very interesting for me, because I was able to program intervals. Let's say I program the ratio 61 to 64. Well, nobody had ever been able to hear it before. No way, impossible. I used to tune these first oscillators that I had back in the '60s using Lissajous patterns. You know what Lissajous patterns are? You use an oscilloscope, and you put one tone in the y-axis and one in the z-axis, and it makes a pattern. If you have a simple ratio like 2 to 1, one axis is horizontal, and the other is vertical;

one axis has two points, and the other has one. Or if you have 3 to 2, one axis has three points, and the other has two. By watching the pattern—they tend to move; in those days oscillators tended to drift. So you would tune them up so that the pattern stood exactly still, and there was then a way if you used the z-axis to count up a pretty high number. I used to count thirty-one segments in the z-axis over a simpler pattern on the x- and y-axis. But this was, like, taking forever, to count up thirty-one points, and with the Rayna synthesizer I can use primes like 127, anything literally within whatever the limit of the thing is—I didn't find out yet. But it definitely has limits, but they could easily be bypassed.

I had, then, the opportunity to listen to intervals that I had never heard before, so that the synthesizer-computer combination then became like a teacher and a model. It offered me something that I had never heard before, and that no one else had ever heard before. So if you go to this environment of mine, for instance, in New York City, one of the things you should know is that it's using prime numbers selected from the range of 288 to 224 in the harmonic series that reduces to the ratio of 9 to 7; 9 to 7 is an interval that I've been interested in for a long time, and, you know, how many people know anything about the harmonic series? OK. Very simply, the harmonic series can be thought of as, my voice is different from your voice, because the harmonics in my voice and in your voice are in different resonant chambers, which emphasize different harmonics. The harmonics don't sound the same because the resonant chamber that they take place in is different, and it emphasizes some of the harmonics in my voice, where in your voice it may not. Some ladies have higher-pitched voices, some men have higher-pitched voices, some have lower-pitched voices, all of these factors go to make up the difference in our voices. But the harmonics, the way the harmonics sound, is one of the very most important things.

The harmonic series is best represented as the positive integers. So they just go 1, 2, 3, 4, 5, 6, 7, 8, 9, 10, 11, 12, up on into, through the series of positive integers. So, the lowest tone is 1, and an octave higher is 2. The very definition of an octave is that it has twice as many frequencies per unit time as the octave below it. The ratio of a perfect fifth is the ratio of 3 to 2. It means you have three frequencies happening in the time of two frequencies. So you have three positive pulses in the time of two positive pulses. As you go through the vowels, you emphasize different harmonics in the voice. To give you an example of why constant frequency helps you to have a more elaborate set of intervallic relationships: If I sing a tone today, and a year later I sing a tone and ask you to compare them, it is very difficult. If I sing one today, and I sing it tomorrow, still not so easy. But, if I sing it now and sing it right after it, it's much better. But the best case is [sings with Marian] if the two are happening simultaneously. The measurement of frequency has to take place in time, and tuning is a function of time. Scientists used to study the movement of planetary bodies for thousands of years and compare what astronomers back in Egypt had recorded, in Greece, and compare these movements over many, many, many years to begin to be able to get a sense of what was really the tuning of a particular planetary body. And, in frequency, it's the same thing. If I give [produces quiet, staccato tones], it's very difficult to get a sense of what its exact pitch is. If I start holding it out [sings], then you can latch onto it, you can start thinking about it, you can study it, and the same is true with instruments. If you analyze the tuning of intervals with instruments, even though instruments are now very fast and they can come up with an instantaneous reading; nonetheless, the reading is more precise if you let it run for a few days, weeks, months, or years than it is if you just do the instantaneous reading. And the drone state of mind that can be established in a *Dream House*, then, can allow your imagination to take new flights of fancy, go in new directions, go in previously untraversed paths, because it has a new set of reference frequencies to which you can be constantly keeping in touch as needed. And, for me, that's one of the interesting things that can take place in a *Dream House*. Yes?

QUESTION

As an experimental musician, could you talk about your experience being an American before a European audience in the musical scene, versus that of being an American before an American audience in the American scene?

LA MONTE YOUNG

As an experimental musician? This is a question very dear to my heart because I think that America's the most creative place in the world. It's very difficult for anybody like me to have ever evolved out of Europe. Tradition is very strong in Europe. We're very young. You know, because we're young, because our forefathers came to this country and literally started over in the woods and made their own way, invented their own safety pin, we're still part of that beginning. And we still have this sense of creativity such that we have to be able to think about it ourselves and do it ourselves. Additionally, because what tradition we had was from so many different places, we developed a sense that, OK, tradition was important, but you could break tradition. In fact, tradition is there for your own good, but you go to Europe and there is only tradition. It's very difficult to get out of tradition. I'll give you the simplest example. I grew up in L.A. In L.A., the supermarkets are open all night long every day of the week. You go to Europe, the stores close at five o'clock, and they are closed—it's over, for the night. They open at eight in the morning, and they close on Saturday at 1:00 p.m., and they never are open on Sunday. Some stores have put up an incredible fight, and they are able to stay open until 8:00 p.m. It's like that on every level.

Young composition students are really fighting the tradition, and in the '60s Europeans thought it was literally inconceivable that a person like me wanted to live in sound environments all the time. They think that, you know, you do some music and then you don't do music and you do something else, and vacations . . . it's the way . . . you know, I haven't had a vacation in maybe some ten years. It's difficult being a composer who earns his living through his work to ever get caught up on money; it's a very difficult situation. So, I don't really have time for vacations. But I am so involved in what I'm doing and so happy, and I do get to go on tour, that I don't ever really exactly want a vacation. Once I had a vacation; somebody insisted I take a vacation in 1985. I took this vacation, and what did we do? We practiced and I composed; I finally had a chance to compose. I am so busy running my life that chances to do creative things are rare. I have to really fight to get a commission, to get some time to get free to compose something, because a lot of my time goes into the production of the work. You produce records, you produce concerts, and you try to keep your work semiarchived.

And so . . . I really like performing in America, but there is one good thing about performing in Europe. And that is that, although we're much more creative here in America, they really think artists are important, unlike what most Americans think. I go to Italy, and they want to touch me. They think I'm important. In America the artist is the lowest possible thing. You go out there into the Midwest—I know, I was born in Idaho. I go back and I visit them once in a while. I've heard guys say, "I don't want any of my tax money going to some faggot in Greenwich Village for some art program." That's what they say. I mean, they're just thinking totally differently from what you and I are thinking about. They haven't yet had an opportunity to learn that art on the highest level is perhaps the most important thing that can lead humanity into a better future. But they have that sense in Europe. Somehow, when we got over to America, life was so hard. During the recession that we had just in these last few years, you have a good example. There was very little support for the arts because people really needed the money to buy a quart of milk. And when push comes to shove, it's basic survival. It's true; you can't eat a painting. You can listen to a good piece of music and it might help your psychological state for a while; but, you know, the basics are the basics: food, water, sex, drugs, rock and roll.

I think that it's very nice to perform in Europe, and it's very nice to have that kind of appreciation, that they actually think you're doing something important, but I love to come back to America because I really think it's the most inspiring, most creative place I've ever been in the entire world. I've been to India, and they're even more middle-class than the United States. Talk about Middle America; these people are so concerned about what their next-door neighbor thinks about them. My God, you know, it's impossible. And for somebody like Pandit Pran Nath to have evolved out of Indian culture, it's practically a miracle, because there's so much against anything that's out of line. Within the realm of music, of course, an enormous amount has been done, and in certain religious traditions in India . . . but nonetheless, just as soon as you get slightly out of that, well. . . . In India, musicians are considered one of the lowest castes.

I think that very few people go through life and end up being like me, ready to break away from it all. You know, I grew up in a very, very strong religious tradition, my entire family was Mormon, and it was their entire life. They went to church seven days a week. Your entire life was programmed, and I was a model student. I had 100 percent attendances for years and years and years. When I left the church when I was seventeen years old, it literally broke the whole family's heart. Why did I leave the church? One of the reasons, to be advanced in the priesthood as a Mormon, you had to believe that the Mormon Church was the only true church. And I went to my interview to be advanced, and I said, "Well, I believe the Mormon Church is true, but I also believe other religions are true, and I definitely don't think this is the only true church." And so that was that. And it was over. But are we nearing the end of the hour?

ALVIN LUCIER

Yes, we are, if we want to perform Poem. I think we could have another question, perhaps.

LA MONTE YOUNG

You choose the next person to ask the question.

ALVIN LUCIER

Mark Slobin, our chairman.

MARK SLOBIN

This might be easy. In terms of Indian music, has your relationship to it evolved in particular ways over the last period?

LA MONTE YOUNG

Well, I had a very traditional training in Indian classical music with Pandit Pran Nath. Marian and I brought Pandit Pran Nath to New York City in January 1970. We became his first American disciples. And he literally wouldn't teach us unless we became disciples. There are different levels of study of Indian classical music. They have students who just come and take lessons and go away, but the disciple goes to a ceremony where—various things take place at the ceremony. A red band is tied around your wrist. And through this ceremony, you take on the responsibility of supporting your teacher throughout life, and he takes on the responsibility of teaching you music. He taught us in an extremely strict way. For instance, some of you know that Marian and I live on a very special rotating sleeping-waking cycle. Currently, we're usually awake for about twenty hours and then we sleep for about ten hours. And this goes around, all the time it's going around. So we have to predict in advance what our schedule's going to be. But during the years that we studied with Pran Nath, he wouldn't let us live on that schedule. He felt that the serious lessons had to take place at sunrise. So, I had to wake every day at three or four and make tea so that tea was ready when he was ready to wake up, and then we would serve him tea, and he would give the lesson. And if he happened to be staying somewhere else, and we had to go to where he was, if we came after 7:00 a.m., he wouldn't teach us. So, he was very strict with us. He would sometimes hit me at the lessons. I was already over thirty years old, thirty-five years old when he was hitting me. His teacher used to beat him in public, and his teacher's teacher had scars on his back where his teacher beat him with an iron rod. And they were some of the greatest musicians of all time. It's really a question of discipline. And, you know, I'm not saying that that's the best way or the only way to teach, but that's how that tradition had been coming down, that you had to really line the students up, the students had to be very serious, they had to be totally devoted.

The one thing about his style, the Kirana style, also known as the style of Krishna, was based on the concept of devotion, and devotion to the teacher was the main thing. No matter what the teacher said, you had to do it. Even if he, like, for instance, one Muslim singer once said to me, Salamat Ali Khan said, "You know, we Muslims, we don't drink, but if the teacher tells you to pour alcohol on the shrine, we have to do it." And so, literally, my studies with Pran Nath completely changed my life in that they introduced an entire new world of music—for instance, you have two different ragas that use the same mode. Yet the way you go from *sa* to *re*, let's say C to D, in these two ragas is completely different—something that was literally unheard of in Western classical music. And additionally, he taught me an entire lifestyle about performing, how to prepare for a performance. On the day of a performance, he would not speak to anybody; he was just totally—his mouth was closed. He didn't want you talking to him, and right up to the performance, this bomb would happen at the concert. Then afterward he'd drink wine. It was just like a revelation to me to live with him, to observe him, to watch him, what made a master Indian vocalist a master. It was literally probably the highest experience of our lives.

When he passed away in California, we were able to spend time with his body in the room. They let us take the body home to his house and let us keep it there for thirty-six hours. It was an incredible spiritual experience that I had not anticipated. We thought we would be very sad, because we had literally studied with him for twenty-six years, and maybe 50 percent of that time we lived with him. This amazing spiritual presentation of him became manifest, and it was literally unbelievable, so I can only thank him for what he gave us, and I thank you for having us here. It's been exciting to be able to talk to you, and I hope I can come again some time. Thank you very much, Alvin.

ALVIN LUCIER

You're welcome. Thank you.

6

STEVE REICH

December 9, 1997

ALVIN LUCIER

Steve Reich is no stranger to Wesleyan; he has been here several times. Years ago, he came up for the summer and took Abraham Adzenyah's African drumming classes. His Steve Reich Ensemble performed a concert in 1974 on the Crowell series. In 1988, the New World Consort performed a concert of his works, including his *Octet.* Several of our graduate students have been members of the Steve Reich Ensemble and have been an integral part of the whole panorama of his music. The hundreds of students who have taken Music 109 know a good deal about his music. I started teaching Steve's work as far back as 1968, when I first came to Wesleyan.

In the late '60s, I was in Antioch, Ohio, performing with the Sonic Arts Union. At that time, David Behrman was producing records for CBS Records. He came into our rehearsal and said, "I'd like to play you something of Steve Reich's that I'm putting on Odyssey [record label]. It's called *Come Out.*" We stopped rehearsing, and he played the piece. We were stunned. It was one of those times when you see or hear something and you know something very new has just occurred, something new and good and important. It was that simple piece that we all know, so I don't have to describe it, in which a speaker's recorded voice moves out of phase with itself, creating a canon. We all know that a canon is an essential form in music, but, in this case, you could hear it being made in real time before your very ears. What a simple and fruitful idea that was. Until the early '70s, Steve made pieces during which identical sound material moves out of phase with itself. Since then, he has expanded that idea, invented many others, and has made a wonderful body of work. Steve Reich is one of the few composers that I know that has been able to maintain the integrity of his ideas and yet make a music that appeals to a lot of people.

STEVE REICH

A couple of weeks ago, I was out in Utah, of all places, and the sponsor said, "I hear you're working on some book of collected writings." And I said, "I am," and he said, "Well, why don't you bring something out here and read it?" And I thought, "Ah, that's a bad idea," but I did it. And it went over pretty well, I think, so I hope I won't bore you. What I'm going to do is read a bunch of really short one- or two-page pieces on different composers probably most of you have heard of. And then you will have heard me lecture. And then with that out of the way, I'm going to play . . . how many people here have heard the piece *Proverb* before? Well, OK. For those of you who've heard it, I've got two scores, because I know you haven't seen the score. The rest of you will hear the piece. It's fourteen minutes. I'm going to talk for about fifteen minutes, fourteen minutes of music, and then I'm just going to answer any questions you've got about anything that I can answer. So here we go.

RE: SCHOENBERG

Arnold Schoenberg's influence in America was quite pronounced during the 1950s and '60s. It was, of course, due to the activities of Stockhausen, Boulez, and Berio at this time that brought renewed interest in Schoenberg's music. Even John Cage was, in many ways, a follower of his teacher Schoenberg, with whom he studied at UCLA, most especially in Cage's rejection of any sort of harmonic organization of musical form. This brought about the situation in the late '50s and early '60s, during which time I was a music student at Juilliard and then at Mills College with Berio, that anyone writing music that was not either serial or aleatoric was simply not worthy of the slightest consideration. Now, about thirty-five years later, what remains musically? Well, of serial music, some works of Boulez, Stockhausen, and Berio, and a few others. Their imitators, particularly in America, appear more or less exactly as what they always were, Americans once again aping their European betters. Even in terms of John Cage, it seems that while his books and essays of the '60s and beyond remained of theoretical interest, his music that is played and admired most, it seems to me, is the percussion and prepared piano works of the '30s and '40s.

There are, it seems, some fundamental problems in Schoenberg's musical thinking. The main problem is this: the reality of cadence to a key or modal center is basic in all the music of the world, Western and non-Western. This reality is also related to the primacy of the intervals of the fifth, the fourth, the octave in all the world's music, as well as the physical acoustics of sound.

Similarly for regular rhythmic pulse. Any theory of music that eliminates these realities is relegated to a marginal role in the music of the world. The postman will never whistle Schoenberg. It's been almost a hundred years, but even two hundred years or more will bring no improvement in this respect. This doesn't mean that Schoenberg was not a great composer. Clearly, he was. It does mean that his music, and all the music like his, will always inhabit a sort of dark corner, off by itself in the history of the world's music. It is thus no accident that his quite understandably most popular works all predate his invention of the twelve-tone system. The piano pieces Op. 11 and 19, the *Five Pieces for Orchestra* Op. 16 (particularly the third movement, "Farben," or "Changing Colors on a Lake"), as well as *Verklärte Nacht*, *Pierrot Lunaire*, etc., will, it seems, remain as his most performed and listened to works. This is not due to a limitation in the intelligence of listeners. It is due to a limitation of Schoenberg's later music.

After Schoenberg, Berg, and Webern came a pause followed by Stockhausen, Boulez, and Berio, and then after them came myself, Riley, Glass, Young, and later many others. This most recent group of composers, of which I am a part, has been involved in something, on the one hand, quite new in terms of musical structure of repetition and slow harmonic change, and, on the other hand, in a process of restoration. That is, the restoring of melody, counterpoint, and harmony in a recognizable but completely new context. That this music should be listened to with interest worldwide, particularly amongst the young, should come as no surprise. That this music arose in part as a complete turning away from Schoenberg and his ideas comes as no surprise either.

RE: JOHN CAGE

In the early 1960s, when I was a young composer working in a new way, my reaction to John Cage was that his direction was clearly not my own. Nevertheless, Cage's ideas about chance procedures were very much in the air, and it seemed necessary to deal with them one way or the other. In 1968, after I had composed *It's Gonna Rain, Come Out, Piano Phase* (which Cage included in his anthology, *Notations*), *Violin Phase*, and other pieces, I wrote in an essay called "Music Is a Gradual Process"—and now I'm quoting myself from this earlier piece: "John Cage has used processes and has certainly accepted their results, but the processes that he used were compositional ones that could not be heard when the piece was performed. The process of using the *I Ching* or imperfections in a sheet of paper to determine musical parameters can't be heard when [a person is] listening to music composed that way. The compositional process and the sounding music have no audible connection. Similarly, in serial music, the series itself is seldom audible. What I'm interested in"—in those days—"is a compositional process and a sounding music that are one and the same thing."

In order to clarify in words what I had done musically before 1968, it was necessary to distinguish it from the dominant musical directions of that time: the European serialism of Stockhausen, Boulez, and Berio, with whom I had studied, and the chance procedures of John Cage. During the late 1960s and early '70s, I had occasional contacts with Cage. We were both in a series of small classes on the computer language FORTRAN, taught by the composer, pianist, and conductor James Tenney. After one of these classes, Cage played a preview of his then new *Cheap Imitation*. Later he came to a private preview performance of my *Drumming*. During this time, I began to appreciate the tenacity and consistency of Cage as a person. My impression of his contribution is basically that his early percussion and prepared piano pieces will survive best. It is sometimes suggested that these early works had laid the groundwork for the kind of music I, and others, wrote in the 1960s and the early '70s, in that Cage's early works were structured rhythmically rather than harmonically. There was clearly some technical affinity between his early work and my own; however, since I never studied Cage's early works at that time, they had no conscious influence on my music.

Over the years, I have come to value those composers who have a distinct voice of their own. There's one over there. [Points to Alvin Lucier]. Talent and technique alone without a distinct vision seem increasingly irrelevant. John Cage had a vision and followed it.

RE: FELDMAN

I didn't hear any of Feldman's music until 1962, when I heard a piece of Stockhausen's called *Refrain*. I only realized later that this was Stockhausen's Feldman piece, just as *Stimmung* was his La Monte Young piece. In 1963, I wrote a piece called *For Three or More Pianos, or Piano and Tape,* which was influenced by *Refrain*, which is to say that it was influenced by Feldman without me even knowing it at the time.

When I moved back to New York from San Francisco in September 1965, I didn't pay much attention to Morton Feldman. I knew he was there, that he was part of the group around John Cage, that his music was quiet, but at that time it was important for me to get away from all of it, from Feldman, Cage, just as from Stockhausen, Berio, and Boulez. In 1971, Feldman and Cage attended a private loft performance of *Drumming.* Later, at a party, Feldman and I had a chance to talk, and from 1971 on we met from time to time. He was, as everyone who knows him or who ever met him [knows], an absolutely unforgettable human being. During that time, he generously told me that my *Four Organs* had made a strong impression on him. Gradually, I became aware of his *Piece for Four Pianos* from 1957, eight years before my own *It's Going to Rain*, which utilized a rhythmically free form of changing phase relations. All four players play from the same score but are free to pass through the chords at their own pace. By the '80s, when Feldman started writing longer pieces, I foolishly didn't take the time to listen to them, and Feldman drifted out of my musical consciousness. And then in 1987, Morty died.

Within the next few years, I began to listen to some of his late works. Two of them, *Piano and String Quartet*, 1985, and *The Turfan Fragments*, particularly struck me. *Piano and String Quartet* is the most beautiful work of his that I know, and upon examining the score, I began to see that many of its quiet, mysterious chords were actually inversions of themselves, repetitions of material that were never exact repetitions. In *The Turfan Fragments*, there is again a play of rhythmic phase relationships within the music. Feldman was able to combine extremely chromatic harmony, soft dynamics, generally slow, flexible tempos with minimal phase and variation techniques. I felt like I was getting a composition lesson from the grave. I wanted to call him to tell him I had missed the boat with his late pieces, to ask him how he made them, but that was no longer possible. I miss Morton Feldman, and I love and admire his music.

RE: BERIO

Before I studied with Luciano Berio at Mills College in California, I heard his *Circles*, a setting of the American poet e. e. cummings, for voice, harp, and percussion. It was sung by Cathy Berberian and conducted by Berio at the New School in New York in about 1960. It was an ear- and mind-opener. I can remember what seemed like numberless sentimental settings of cummings in the 1950s by American composers whose names I can't remember. In contrast, here was an Italian who clearly understood that cummings's poetry was largely about the individual syllables of which it was made. The first syllable of the word "stinging," which separated—this is in Berio's setting—into a very long-held "ssss" followed by "ting" and finally "ing," by the soprano, whose sibilance on the "ssss" was answered by two sandpaper blocks rubbed together by a percussionist. The marriage of instrumental timbre with syllabic timbre went exactly to the heart of cummings's poetry. It was a lesson in setting a text without the need of a classroom.

When I studied with Berio from 1961–63 at Mills, he early on played a tape of his piece *Omaggio a Joyce,* which showed again how speech, often broken down into the syllables of *Finnegans Wake*, could be a riveting source for tape music as well. It was more interesting to me, by far, than the tape pieces made with electronically generated tones, and it encouraged me later on, in 1965 and '66, with my own speech-tape pieces *It's Going to Rain*, and *Come Out*.

As a composition student with Berio, I continued to use the twelve-tone rows, as I had done since 1960, while still at Juilliard. My procedure was not to transpose, not to invert, not to retrograde the row, but to repeat it over and over again. Berio saw a three-minute string orchestra piece—a student piece of mine, which I had written at Juilliard—that used a repeated row throughout. He said, "If you want to write tonal music, why don't you write tonal music?" I said, "That's what I'm trying to do." Berio's straight-to-the-point response helped me on my way. I thank him for that, and for his music.

RE: KURT WEILL, THE ORCHESTRA, AND VOCAL STYLE — AN INTERVIEW WITH K. ROBERT SCHWARTZ (1992)

K. ROBERT SCHWARTZ
Why didn't you write a music theater piece before *The Cave*?

STEVE REICH

Actually, I was asked to write operas during the '80s, first by the Holland Festival and then by the Frankfurt Opera. Both times I said no. At the time, I knew that I didn't want to spend several years writing a conventional opera since I had some misgivings about the form itself. What really opened the door to opera for me was *Different Trains.* I began to realize that if you could see people speaking on videotape and at the same time see and hear live musicians literally playing their speech melodies, that would be a perfect place for me to begin a new kind of opera or music theater.

K. ROBERT SCHWARTZ

Did you have any models in the history of opera or music theater?

STEVE REICH

The most useful historical model for me turns out to be Kurt Weill. What I learned from him is that if you're going to write a piece of music theater, there are two basic questions you're obliged to ask yourself. What and where is the orchestra? And, two, what is the vocal style? Weill is a student of Busoni and as a working composer could have chosen the standard orchestra in the pit when he did *The Threepenny Opera,* but no, he chose a banjo, saxophone, trap drums, the cabaret ensemble. As for the vocal style, again, given his background, it would have been natural to assume that he wanted a bel canto operatic voice. Again, he said no, and he chose a woman with a rough cabaret voice. The result is a masterpiece that completely captures its historical time; not the time of Mozart or Verdi or Wagner, it captures the Weimar Republic. And it does this precisely because of his choice of orchestra and vocal style.

In my case, I have since 1987 felt that the standard symphony orchestra is not my orchestra. It's the orchestra of Wagner and Mahler and the rest of the German Romantics. My own orchestra is usually less than twenty musicians, and I only need one player to a part, with amplification making possible balances between, say, solo strings and percussion. If you add more strings, they lose their rhythmic agility and develop a kind of overweight timbre that is inappropriate to what I'm trying to do. The amplification is not there as a kind of Band-Aid for poor orchestration; it's there because that is the one and only way to get the sound that I need for the music that I write. Similarly with vocal style. Historically, the bel canto voice in a Mozart opera had to be heard over an orchestra of something like thirty to forty musicians, and we think of that now as a light operatic voice, even though it had to be heard over all those musicians and often in a large hall. By the time we get to Wagner, he has expanded the brass section enormously, and it is necessary to make a corresponding expansion in the number of strings to balance the brass. Hence, in Wagner opera the singer needs a huge voice just in order to be heard. In both cases, the vocal style is linked with the basic acoustical realities of sound volume coming from the orchestra.

Well, about one hundred years ago, the microphone was invented, and it then became possible to sing in a more intimate way with a small, more natural voice and still be heard over very large ensembles, very loud ensembles, woodwinds, brass, percussion, and what have you. This is, in fact, the kind of voice that I grew up hearing in popular music, jazz, and later rock. The acoustical realities changed with the microphone, and the vocal style changed with it.

K. ROBERT SCHWARTZ

Are you saying that composers should avoid using the orchestra and bel canto voices if they write an opera?

STEVE REICH

Certainly not, *if* they have a reason to use them. For instance, Stravinsky, in *The Rake's Progress*, is making his comment on Mozart opera, and even Auden's libretto, based on Hogarth, is eighteenth century in subject and tone. Stravinsky needed a classical orchestra, and he specifies only double winds and brass, no trombones or tuba, with a cembalo part to be played by the piano. This was the necessary orchestra for him to recreate his eighteenth-century opera. Similarly, the vocal style in *The Rake's Progress* is usually sung by the kinds of singers who sing in Mozart opera. A totally different example would be John Cage's *Europera*. Here Cage was manipulating, through chance, procedures material drawn directly from the standard operatic literature. He obviously needed the orchestra and vocal style of the standard repertoire to achieve this. What I'm objecting to is a more or less unconscious or knee-jerk assumption on the part of composers today that opera equals bel canto voices on stage and orchestra in the pit. If it makes sense for what you're trying to achieve, fine, but if your opera is about characters who lived anywhere from the 1930s to the present and then you unquestioningly have your singers sing as if they stepped out of eighteenth- or nineteenth-century Germany or Italy, you create a superficial and inadvertently foolish and amusing situation. If you are writing an opera about, say, General Eisenhower and he appeared singing as if he stepped out of *The Marriage of Figaro*, that could well be seen as a joke. It would be altogether more serious and genuinely more engaging to have him sing like Frank Sinatra, and instead of an orchestra in the pit, why not a complete Glenn Miller band on stage?

K. ROBERT SCHWARTZ

So you see Kurt Weill as pointing the way to the future?

STEVE REICH

Definitely. Look at his musical context. Berg composed *Wozzeck* in 1921 with a huge orchestra and large vocal style, and one can certainly see his work as done under the shadow of the death of German romanticism. Weill was aware of that death, but his reaction in 1928 is *The Threepenny Opera*. While Berg is looking backward, Weill instead does an about-face and looks to contemporary popular forms as material for his musical theater.

K. ROBERT SCHWARTZ

One of Weill's concerns throughout his life was in combining materials from popular culture with those of European high culture. In effect, he blurred the supposed divide between the two. Does that have special meaning for you?

STEVE REICH

We are living in a time now when the worlds of concert music and popular music have resumed their dialogue. Perhaps I've had a hand in this restoration myself, but certainly Kurt Weill began it long before I was born. This dialogue, of course, is the normal way of the musical world. The French popular song of the fifteenth century, "Missa L'homme armé," served as the cantus firmus of more than thirty masses composed by the likes of Du Fay, Ockeghem, Josquin des Prez, and Palestrina. Later, from about 1600 to the death of J. S. Bach, the instrumental suite is based on stylizations of actual dances of a somewhat earlier period, often including allemande, courante, sarabande, and gigue, amongst others. The use of folk song by later composers includes, amongst others, Beethoven in the Sixth Symphony, Bartók and Kodaly in many of their compositions, and Stravinsky in *The Rite of Spring, The Firebird*, and *Les Noces*. It seems that the wall between serious and popular music was erected primarily by Schoenberg and his followers. Since the late 1960s, this wall has gradually crumbled, and we are back, more or less, to the normal situation where concert musicians and popular musicians take a healthy interest in what their counterparts have done and are doing. Kurt Weill pointed the way back in the 1920s.

ALVIN LUCIER

Before we move on to questions, let's listen to a surprise performance of Steve's recent *Vermont Counterpoint*, played by visiting flute teacher Peter Standaart.

STEVE REICH

I didn't even know this performance was going to happen until Alvin told me about it yesterday. But I'm glad because it's always much better to hear something that we all can share.

Before I take your questions, I'd like to thank Alvin Lucier for inviting me but more importantly for his enormous contribution to contemporary music. I'm sure you've all heard his *I Am Sitting in a Room,* and I imagine you all appreciated the depth of honesty and musical invention in that piece. When I first heard it in 1970 at the Guggenheim Museum, my first thought was "Incredible! Why didn't I think of that?" Well, I didn't think of that because I'm not Alvin. He was able to turn speech into music by re-recording his own voice until his vowels combined with, as he says, the "resonant frequencies of the room," to turn his words into a kind of ghostly sitar. For me, the key sentence is: "I regard this activity not so much as a demonstration of a physical fact, but more as a way to smooth out any irregularities my speech may have." Alvin shows that whatever the brilliance of your musical ideas, they will most likely reach others if they carry your personal conviction with them. Now, any questions?

QUESTION

What are your opinions about contemporary electronic dance music?

STEVE REICH

Thank you, and I hope you'll bear with a long answer. When I was a kid, I took piano lessons, and on recordings I listened to Beethoven's Fifth, Schubert's *Unfinished*, the overture to *Der Meistersinger*, Broadway shows, pop music of the day, and so on. In other words, no classical music before Haydn or after Wagner, and no real jazz. It wasn't until the age of fourteen that I heard *The Rite of Spring,* the Fifth *Brandenburg Concerto*, and bebop—Charlie Parker, Miles Davis, and drummer Kenny Clarke. These three musics changed my life. I'm still under their influence. At that time, I had a friend who was a better pianist than I was, and we wanted to start a band. I said, "I'm the drummer," and started taking snare drum lessons from Roland Kohloff, the best local drummer who ended up being timpanist with the New York Philharmonic. I also began going down to Birdland on 52nd Street to hear Miles Davis and Kenny Clarke—Charlie Parker died before I could hear him—and it made an enormous impression on me. Later on, when I was studying composition at Juilliard and then Mills, roughly between 1960 and 1964, I must have heard John Coltrane play forty or fifty times live in New York and in San Francisco. He was playing what was called "modal jazz," which, in a nutshell, was based on very few chords. In *Africa/Brass*, for example, he stays on E, from the low E string on the bass, for over sixteen minutes. All that in 1961, before Riley, me, or Glass.

That was a huge influence musically, and, if you like, morally. I was going to school at that time at Mills College and studying with Luciano Berio. Most of the student composers were writing incredibly complex pieces, and they weren't playing them on any instrument. I had serious doubts whether they heard those pieces in their heads. So that was my daytime activity; at night I would go hear Coltrane. He would pick up his soprano or tenor sax, and the music would just come out. Facing that dichotomy, I decided that with whatever limitations I have, I have to play in my own pieces. So, I would say that jazz influenced the rhythmic feel of what I do, and it also made me a player in my own ensemble.

Now, you asked about contemporary electronic dance music. Maybe I can at least get close to answering. Let's go back to 1974, London, Queen Elizabeth Hall, and my ensemble's giving a concert. Concert's over, a guy comes up with lipstick, long hair, and says, "How do you do? I'm Brian Eno." Then, in 1976, my ensemble gave the German premiere of *Music for 18 Musicians* at the National Gallery in Berlin, and David Bowie was there. In 1978, the piece was released on the ECM jazz label, even though it was recorded for Deutsche Grammophon, because Manfred Eicher, founder of ECM Records, wanted to release it. In New York, ECM was run by Bob Hurwitz, who now runs Nonesuch, and he said, "Look, we'd like you to play this piece at The Bottom Line cabaret club in New York." I said, "Great." David Bowie came again. Then cut to about four or five years ago, again in London, and someone's interviewing me for a pop electronic keyboard magazine, and he asks, "Have you heard The Orb's *Little Fluffy Clouds*?" I said no, and he gave me the CD. I listened and heard that it had fifteen or twenty seconds of *Electric Counterpoint*, the piece I wrote for Pat Metheny. I thought, "Hmmm, these people don't just like what I do, they sample it and put it in their music." I didn't take any legal action, which was a wise decision. Recently, someone gave me some Aphex Twin to listen to. My eighteen-year-old cousin is plying me with techno stuff. It's not Donna Summer, I know. There's discussion now of the possibility of some of these guys doing a remix album of some of my things, and I think it would be great if that happened. There has been a dialogue, back and forth, for a very long time. Composers from Du Fay to Palestrina wrote "Missa L'homme armé" on the French folk song. Haydn's 104th symphony uses an Austrian drinking song. The first movement of Beethoven's fourth uses a folk song. Bartók was so immersed in Serbo Croatian folk music that he collected and analyzed that, even in his string quartets; it's sometimes impossible to single out what is or is not folk material. Stravinsky denied it at times, but Richard Taruskin has shown exactly how *The Rite of Spring* uses Russian folk material. Kurt Weill's *Threepenny Opera* is more Weimar Republic cabaret than traditional opera. Is Gershwin a songwriter or concert composer? Clearly, he's both. Ives constantly uses the Hymn tunes he played as a church organist in *Three Places in New England* and many other works. That's the way it's always been, and unfortunately it was just in this odd little period, when I was a music student the way you are now, when there was the idea that you may enjoy jazz or rock, but it has nothing to do with what you're doing. What you compose must come out of Boulez, Stockhausen, or Cage, or you will definitely not be taken seriously. No harmony, no melody, and certainly no periodic rhythm. That's not in line with the history of Western music, where so much comes out of folk roots. And folk roots in our day . . . You go to a music store, what do you see in the window? You see samplers, digital delays, et cetera. That's our urban folk music. You can hate it, you can love it, you can do what you like, but it's a fact. It would be odd if it didn't have some effect on "serious" or classical composers. In America, that's our tradition. Charles Ives, George Gershwin, Aaron Copland, and so much since. It's our heritage, our stomping ground, and you can do what you want about it, but you must be aware of it.

QUESTION

What are you listening to?

STEVE REICH

I have a tremendous admiration for Arvo Pärt. Also, I'm very interested in the music of Michael Gordon, who is a member of the Bang on a Can group. His *Yo Shakespeare* and *Trance* are available on recording. A brand new one called *Love Bead* sounds like Michael Gordon meets Igor Stravinsky, *The Rite of Spring*, particularly. I'm interested in *Cheating, Lying, Stealing* by David Lang. I strongly recommend that to you. I'm also interested in Louis Andriessen's *de Staat* and *Hoketus*.

QUESTION

Both pieces that we've heard today remind me strongly of the composer David Bordon, and I wondered if you've had any interaction with him or know his work at all?

STEVE REICH

Yes, David's at Cornell. He was in the dance department, but now he's in the music department. He formed Mother Mallard's Portable Masterpiece Group years ago. Nurit Tilles from my ensemble was drafted to be one of his keyboard players. I met David about the time when the *It's Gonna Rain* album was being recorded at Columbia, in the late 1960s. It made an impression on him, and later Philip Glass made an impression on him. David is one of a number of younger people for whom my generation—the Terry Riley, Steve Reich, Phil Glass generation—has had an effect.

QUESTION

How would you capsulize your experience as an American composer connecting with the rest of the world? Over the time that you've come up, from the '60s on, how has your relationship with what's happening in Europe, Eastern Europe, and non-Western countries developed?

STEVE REICH

Well, as far as the European side of it goes, it's an interesting question. Twenty years ago, to get a good performance of my music in Europe would have been virtually impossible. When *The Desert Music* was played in 1984 by the Cologne Radio Orchestra, it was a disaster. There was no way of informing them of the style of the music. But now—I just literally came back yesterday from Dijon, a small town where the mustard comes from—they got me there for performances of my music by percussion students from Strasbourg—eighteen, nineteen, twenty, and twenty-one years old. And, man, they just tore through my *Sextet, Music for Pieces of Wood,* and *Six Marimbas*—first-rate, intense, serious. It was gorgeous. It's another generation. I also just came back from presenting the second collaboration Beryl Korot and I are making together of a piece called *Hindenburg*, which is being premiered by the Ensemble Modern, a German ensemble. They're similar to the Ensemble InterContemporain in Paris, the London Sinfonietta, the Klangforum Wien, the Avanti Ensemble in Scandinavia, and the Asko Schoenberg Ensemble in Holland. Ensembles like these are growing like mushrooms all over Europe. They consist of from fifteen to forty musicians, well funded, full-time gigs, recording contracts, tours. They decide what they want to play, who their conductor's going to be, what their repertoire is going to be, and they have their own audio engineer as part of the group. They are conservatory-trained musicians but know rock and roll, jazz, some gamelan, and African drumming. It's a new breed of European musicians; they play my music and that of my contemporaries completely idiomatically.

As to European composers, I mentioned that I am very interested in Arvo Pärt and also Louis Andriessen. I also have a high regard, as so many others do, for Ligeti, including *Atmosphères*, *Clocks and Clouds*, and his piece for one hundred metronomes. Finally, I was a student of Luciano Berio, from whom I learned that human speech, rather than electronically generated sound, was the great source for tape music. As for non-Western music, you may know that I was a student of both Ghanaian drumming and Balinese Gamelan back in the 1970s. I learned a great deal from both that definitely encouraged me to continue composing, as I began to in 1965.

There's a new recording of *Music for 18 Musicians* on BMG by the Ensemble Modern in Frankfurt, with guest artists Russell Hartenberger and Bob Becker, who got their doctorates here at Wesleyan. It was like passing the torch, in a sense, to another ensemble. They had the written materials, and we gave them the oral tradition.

QUESTION

Can you explain what was happening in the first piece?

STEVE REICH

Vermont Counterpoint? It consists basically of canons. It is written for garden-variety instruments; in other words, flute, alto flute, and piccolo. I didn't want to write for bass flute because I tend to shy away from instruments that almost nobody has. It began when flutist Ransom Wilson asked me to write him a concerto. I told him I didn't write concertos; I'm not interested in the idea of a solo line against an orchestra or a chamber orchestra. Then I thought to myself, "This guy's a great player, there ought to be something I can do." So I called him back and said, "Would you be interested in performing a piece that would be like those earlier pieces I did back in the '60s in which you play against prerecordings of yourself?" To my surprise, he said yes, and I wrote *Vermont Counterpoint* for him. There's also a piece called *New York Counterpoint* for clarinets, which has recently been recorded by Evan Ziporyn, a member of the Bang on a Can All-Stars. It was written for clarinets and bass clarinet; it's got a bigger sound.

Then there's *Electric Counterpoint* with Pat Metheny playing guitars and electric basses. If you orchestrated *Vermont Counterpoint* for flute, clarinet, and oboe, for example, you wouldn't get that web of sound. This is true for all these counterpoint pieces: I'm playing a line, you're playing a line, she's playing a line, and we want to play them in different rhythmic positions and get this web of sound, where you're not sure if it is me or the other player. You get that in *Piano Phase*, too. To achieve this you've got to have identical timbres so that the individual voices blend and form one web of interlocking melodic patterns. If you had flute, clarinet, and oboe, you would have a totally different and—in this kind of music—unsuccessful result. The basic thing is that they must be consorts of identical instruments playing unison canons.

QUESTION

Could you comment on the influences of Arvo Pärt on the piece *Proverb*?

STEVE REICH

It's a fair question, but the answer is none. When I was a music student at Cornell and William Austin was teaching music history, he played one of the first pieces of four-part counterpoint that we have in Western music. That is a four-part organum by Pérotin, *Viderunt Omnes,* from the eleventh century. It made a strong impression on me and made me think seriously about augmentation as a powerful musical technique. My piece *Four Organs* from back in 1970 would have been impossible without Pérotin. You ask about *Proverb*, and the answer is I wrote it with the score of Pérotin's *Viderunt Omnes* on my piano. The piece is an homage to Pérotin and was written for Paul Hillier and his early music group, Theater of Voices. Arvo Pärt is another composer, amongst several others nowadays, who is more interested in the period of music, let's say from 1100 to 1750, than they are in the period between 1750 to 1900. So in that sense, Pärt and I share that. Have any of you heard *Tehillim*, a piece of mine, a setting of the Psalms, sung by early music singers? I've been working with early music singers since *Music for 18 Musicians.* They just blend into the fabric of my music; *Proverb* really wears it on its sleeve. It conjures up the same associations as Pärt's music does, because he also deals with the vocabulary of church chant of which Pérotin is one of first great innovators. It's a fair question.

QUESTION

The piece for flute and prerecorded flutes evoked the idea of a number of lines in a weave and also the idea of a sort of concerto in that there is a soloist visually performing before us whose timbre is somewhat different than what we hear on the recording. And the ambiance of the occasion is somewhat like that of a flute quartet, somewhat like that of a concerto, and somewhat like that of a recording studio in which somebody is laying down the last track. Do you have ideas about the nature of the performance event in relation to those different interpretations of it?

STEVE REICH

Primarily, *Vermont Counterpoint* was written for a flute soloist as a very different kind of recital piece. They would be playing solo flute music, or perhaps flute and piano, and then *Vermont Counterpoint* would be quite a change of pace. You do accurately note the kinds of associations one might have by watching and listening to a performance. However, none of those associations were on my mind when I wrote the piece. I just wrote for the flute, alto flute, and piccolo soloist and the prerecorded tracks. Perhaps the association you mention might make experiencing a live performance more interesting. I never try to anticipate what a listener will think while listening. My sole criterion is: if I love it, perhaps you will. You might also find it quite different if you saw and heard a completely live performance of this piece by eleven flutists; that happens fairly often, particularly at music conservatories where there are so many flute students. *Vermont Counterpoint* for flute is the first of a series of counterpoint pieces: *New York Counterpoint* for clarinet and bass clarinet and tape for Richard Stoltzman and *Electric Counterpoint* for electric guitars, electric basses and tape for Pat Metheny. The basic idea of writing an unusual and highly effective recital piece for a soloist was the main focus. In all these cases there have been all live performances here and abroad, particularly at music schools. My feeling is—whatever works. All the things that you suggested are true. There's the concerto aspect, the recording studio, and please add the communal, "Let's get together and play eleven flutes." Your associations would be quite different, I suspect, if you were at one of these performances with no prerecording whatsoever.

QUESTION

I have a question about your essay on Schoenberg. You use a few key examples of folk melodies and folk dance forms to call Bach, Beethoven, and even Stravinsky populist composers and place your music in this history of Western music that remains almost entirely intact except for the exclusion of the Second Viennese School. And you confine them to what you call a dark little corner, presumably hiding away from the sort of populist, what you call the comfortably new light of populist minimalist music . . .

STEVE REICH

I never used the word *populist*. I talked about the folk roots of music. *Populist* is one of those journalistic words like *minimalism* that I don't like to use. I leave that to journalists and academics. Also, I said "dark corner," not "little dark corner." Time will tell, but I would suggest that when Schoenberg said that in fifty years the postman would be whistling his melodies, he was extremely out of touch with musical reality. It's over one hundred years, and I don't think there's a qualifying postman in sight. I believe Schoenberg *was* a great composer, and my personal favorites are "Farben" from Opus 16; Opus 11; and Opus 19. I can't name any of the twelve-tone works I want to hear again. But it's up to you.

QUESTION

Point well taken, but I'm wondering why you go so far out of your way to exclude Schoenberg and his students from this lineage of Western music that you consider yourself such an important part of.

STEVE REICH

I don't exclude them at all. I believe that Schoenberg chose one possible and well-founded response to Wagner's extreme tonal ambiguity. He felt the need, after his own even more chromatic and, I believe, often highly successful pieces, to find a way of dropping harmony entirely as his structural tool and turned to the twelve-tone row. I'm just guessing that, if you were to go through all the orchestral program booklets of the world's orchestras in the last fifteen years and look under the name Schoenberg, you're going to find that Opus 16, *Five Pieces for Orchestra,* is done now and then. And if you look under chamber music programs, you will find *Pierrot Lunaire*, and if you look at piano music, you will find Maurizio Pollini and other pianists playing Opus 11 and Opus 19 and the *Suite for Piano*, Opus 25. You will find less of his other pieces. I love Webern. He's a unique genius. But because of the language that he and Berg and Schoenberg chose, because of the way musical theory in Germany went in this curious direction, it created a barrier for most listeners. Dropping harmony was a huge decision and it seems the twelve-tone row may not have been an adequate substitute. It's not a condemnation; it's an explanation. Most important, note that Debussy, also faced with the enormous influence of Wagner, chose to create a new harmonic language using new scales and modes. This in turn had an effect on Stravinsky, and even Bartók, and, eventually, via Nadia Boulanger, on Aaron Copland and other Americans of his generation. It is from this "French connection" that what you call minimalism derives.

ALVIN LUCIER

Thank you for being here. It was a pleasure.

7

MEREDITH MONK

December 7, 1999

ALVIN LUCIER

I first heard Meredith Monk in 1975 in the Merce Cunningham dance studio in New York. In those days, Merce used to program *Events*, mixes of various dances he had made. He would invite musicians to come in and do anything they wanted.

Meredith was sitting at an electric piano (organ, I guess) and began to sing. It sounded like every woman in the world singing at the same time. That's the way I think of it now, maybe that's a little embarrassing. Then she'd sing another song in another voice, and it still sounded like every woman singing. It was fractal. One voice didn't mean only one thing, they all were exemplifying women's singing. This was before we got interested in world singing styles. It was amazing. I thought to myself, "What is this?" I'd never heard anything like this before in my life. It was one of those amazing shocks you get when you experience something new and wonderful for the first time. You are very lucky if you have that experience once in your lifetime.

Over the years, as I have attended many of Meredith's events and watched her films, I have tried to get a handle on what she was doing with the various arts. Could her work be categorized as multimedia or mixed media? It was very different from anyone else. Merce Cunningham and John Cage would keep dance, music, and decor completely separate. Martha Graham would choreograph to the music of Aaron Copland, for example. With Meredith's work, it seemed that parts of the work that belonged to one art were being composed with the rules and principles of another. In the theater work, *Education of the Girlchild*, an actor would pick up a cup of tea, then put it down, and then do it again several times. It looked like a visual representation of a Mozart symphony, the way the event repeated. I could talk all night, which, of course, I know you would be delighted to hear, but I'll stop now. Here is Meredith Monk.

MEREDITH MONK

First, I'd like so much to thank Alvin Lucier, who is not only my old friend but one of the most inspiring composers in the world and of all time. I'm very touched. Thank you for saying those things, Alvin. And I'm very happy to be here, back at Wesleyan again. I was here about ten years ago.

I thought that what I would do is give you a little bit of background, talk a little bit, and then spend some time singing. After that, I'd be very happy to answer any questions.

So, I'm going to go back to my mom. Thank you, Mom, for having me. I came from a very musical family. My great-grandfather was a cantor in Russia. His son, Joseph Zellman, first came to the New York area but ended up founding and directing a music conservatory in Meriden, Connecticut. He was a Russian bass baritone, came to America on a music scholarship, ended up staying here, concertizing in New York with a contralto in places like the Brooklyn Academy and Carnegie Hall. He founded a music conservatory up in Washington Heights. He married an American pianist, Rose Kornicker. They performed on some of the early Thomas Edison cylinder recordings for voice and piano. I remember his voice very well—a deep, beautiful Russian bass baritone. My mother sang popular music on the radio and also sang jingles. She was the original Muriel Cigar and sang for Blue Bonnet Margarine, Schaefer Beer, Chiquita Banana, Royal Pudding, Robert Hall Clothes, and others.

Basically, my childhood was very much like Woody Allen's *Radio Days*. I would often come with her for jobs. At that time, we were living in Queens. In those days, everything was performed live; there wasn't any tape. Her main job was the *DUZ Does Everything* commercial every day at one o'clock. It was a commercial for a soap opera called *The Road of Life*. Sometimes I would sit on the organist's lap and watch the actors with their scripts, playing their characters; sometimes I would be in the control room drawing on the back of scripts.

So music was definitely a part of my childhood. It was taken for granted. I've been told that I sang before I talked and read music before I read words. Our house had a very aural kind of atmosphere. We sang while washing the dishes and as part of daily life. My mother, my sister, and I sang songs in three-part harmony in the car.

I started piano at a young age and played pretty much through childhood. Although I was never a great pianist, I could sight-read quickly. Because I have a visual challenge called strabismus, where I cannot fuse two images out of my two eyes, I had a kind of left-right lack of coordination. When I was three, my mother heard about classes at Steinway Hall taught by two Polish sisters, the Rohms, in Dalcroze Eurhythmics. Eurhythmic is a technique invented by Jaques-Dalcroze, a Swiss composer and teacher in the late nineteenth century, to teach music and rhythm through body movement. His method was comprised of three components: rhythmic movement exercises in space, solfège, and improvisation. Many conductors have studied it so that they can learn to conduct one rhythm with one hand and another one with the other. He once said that all musical truth can be found in the body.

Most of the children in the class learned the music through the rhythmic movement, but for me, it was more of a way of learning physical coordination and body movement through music, something that I felt [was] very comfortable and familiar. I *loved* it. In a way it was really the beginning of something that I always take for granted, which is that sound is in space and that the voice and the body are one thing. You might learn a scale, but you would do it with your arms as well as hearing it. You might see what it looked like as notes, then you might sing it and clap or dance to it—all the senses working together. That principle has been something that has been at the heart of what I do. I always think that my voice dances and my body sings and that there's really no separation between the two.

That was the beginning of my movement background. I took ballet when I was ten. I was never really a great technical dancer, but I loved to move. At Sarah Lawrence I created what came to be called a combined performing arts program. In the voice department, I studied classical technique, lieder, vocal chamber music, and opera workshop. At the same time, I was composing short pieces for piano. In the dance department, I was studying dance composition and technique. I started working on pieces while I was still at school, where I began to have glimpses of how to put some of these elements together, how to weave voice and movement together and include visual images, objects, and light. For me it was [a] kind of emotional integration. How do you put all these aspects or layers into one form?

Early on I also realized that—because the world that we live in is so complex—that to separate art forms seems to not be really reflective of that world. Western European traditions are the only art that separates these elements. Music is over here, movement is over here, whereas there are so many other forms (as a lot of you students know), Asian theater and African forms, where these elements of music, movement, and theater are combined. No one in those societies really thinks that's such an unusual thing. I find, as time goes by, that actually now it seems to be even more difficult to get past this category thing. It's as if the walls have gotten higher, but I think my big struggle over the years has been to explain that these elements are all part of perception, that, as human beings, we have an incredible, rich perceptual palette that includes all the senses, thought, feeling—everything and anything. And so, to be able to attest to the richness of human beings as performers and also as audience members is something, to me, very affirmative and reflective of the complexity of life. Early on, I realized that this inclusiveness as a philosophical basis for making work was something that was very essential.

I came to New York in the fall of 1964 and first made solo pieces in galleries, churches, alternative spaces. There were a lot of wonderful performance spaces opening up at that time. I would say that my early works were gestural pieces, with cinematic structures—as in what Alvin said, taking principles that might be in another art form and transforming them. How would you make a piece of movement or gesture with the kind of cuts or washes or dissolves that you can work with in film, taking that syntax and seeing what that would be in another form? My soundtracks were on tape that I played live. At that time, we didn't have multitrack tape recorders, but I had a two-track machine and with that I could add different generations of sound by recording on that machine, overlaying more tracks or another one, and even more back on my original one.

At a certain point, after having been in New York for about a year, I started missing singing. I somehow always knew that I wasn't going to be a classical singer because something about it made me feel limited; it just didn't feel right. I had been a folk singer in junior high and high school in Stamford, Connecticut. (One of my friends from second grade in Stamford is in the audience tonight. We sang "Bye Bye Love" together in junior high school.) I partially earned my way through Sarah Lawrence by singing and playing guitar at children's birthday parties.

Because I missed singing so much, I began sitting at a piano and working on regular classical vocal exercises. This was around the mid-1960s, long before most of you were born. One day I started vocalizing, and suddenly I had a revelation that the voice could have the flexibility of the spine, it could have the articulation of a hand. It could have within it male and female, all ages. It could delineate landscapes and characters and have within it limitless colors and timbres, ways of producing sound, range, kinetic impulses. It didn't need words. It was an eloquent language in itself. So basically I started working with myself as a guinea pig and, in some ways—because I had done choreography where I was using my own body—making my material on my own body. I knew how to explore and work with my voice. In some ways, I was lucky that I didn't have physical facility because I had to invent my own style of movement. I could easily transfer that method to working with my voice. And because of my family background, I had a wide range and a strong flexible instrument to start out with. So basically I worked with my own voice and kept on exploring it deeply from that point on.

And that has been very much the center and the heart of what I do. I always say that my work is like a tree with two main branches. One is working and writing music for the voice, for myself and for my ensemble, doing concerts and making CDs. The other branch consists of multidisciplined composite forms, including musical theater pieces and films. Now I've also become interested in making installations that include music and video.

Those are forms that combine sight and sound, that either weave together these elements or maybe put them in counterpoint with each other. I work very much like a mosaicist. I work on one aspect, say the "red" tiles first; then I might discover the "blue" tiles, then "yellow." How does this balance out? How does this make a form or a whole? How does the eye balance out the ear? How do these things work together? Sometimes I'll have an idea for something then wait a long time to figure out what would be the most eloquent form. I like to work in film from time to time because of the flexibility of time and space that you cannot achieve in a live performance. You can really fly from one place to another, or you imply simultaneous time by intercutting. Actually, in live performance you can literally have simultaneous events, and that is something you can't do in film unless you divide the screen into parts.

I believe very deeply in live performance. It's something that I've been fighting for in the world of computers. There's something about a live performance that you just can't get anywhere else. It's the vulnerability of the person. The performer's on a tightrope and could fall off at any time. He or she can make a mistake. It's that figure eight of energy that goes between the performer and the audience that's so special and the communal aspect of a large group of people together and a time and place to be able to let go of that "yack yack" constant narration of experience that we have in our minds. Live performance offers the possibility of having a little silence and space to experience something directly and deeply. That's very healing to people and the world that we're living in. And in that way, I feel that art *is* very healing.

Let me tell you a little bit about one or two other ideas before I talk about some other things that I have been working on. After a few years of being in New York, I started getting tired of the basic proscenium stage situation. I started making pieces outdoors or using large groups of people in architectural spaces. I made a piece called *Juice*. The first part of it was in the Guggenheim Museum. I had a choir of about eighty singers—*singer-movers*—that were performing on the ramps in the building, with the audience looking up. It had a cathedral-like quality and used the resonance of that room, which has a very long decay.

I was very interested in cutting through the habitual pattern of going to see something, having a cup of coffee and talking about it, then forgetting about it. That's the usual ritual of going to a performance. I was trying to make something, for example, that would start on one day, continue a month after that, then a month after that, so that memory became a part of it. Part One of *Juice* started at the Guggenheim Museum, but you bought one ticket for the three different parts. In the Guggenheim there were about nine main cast people along with the chorus. Four of them were painted red from head to toe and were stomping around in big red combat boots. They were only one part of the huge tapestry in the Guggenheim. A month later, you focused more on those four people. A month after that, you went to a gallery and you saw the eighty-five red combat boots that were from the Guggenheim part. You saw the costumes and all the elements that had been in those other two parts, but you could go very close to them. Yet at the same time, the four main characters were on video, so you saw their faces very close, but there were actually no people there. The whole three-part piece was like a giant zoom lens of attention and perception, but, ironically, in the third installation part you got farther and farther away from the people.

I was working very much with these different notions of distance, time, scale, and the relationship of audience to performer. Sometimes I would present performances in the morning or outside in parking lots in New York. I still try to do those site-specific works as much as possible. I did a piece a few years ago on Roosevelt Island where we bussed the audience from one part of the island to the other and worked with a fairly large group of people, including some of the people from the hospitals there.

That's been one strand of my work. The other has been musical theater pieces and opera. I've always called my big pieces operas because they include all these different forms. I did compose an opera called *ATLAS* at a real opera house for the Houston Grand Opera, which was a very interesting experience for me. I worked on it for five years. Part of the process was the rehearsal period, when I taught my way of working to singers who came from a classical background, and I soon realized that rhythmic articulation and complexity as well as working with the voice in different ways was not part of their experience. I had to figure out what I could do for them. I chose people who were open minded and willing to play and were not too rigid in their ideas of what singing was about.

So basically, this is what I've done all these years. I keep on moving along from one step to the next. For about the last fifteen years I've done a Buddhist meditation practice that has been very helpful for me in many ways. The first thing is how I work with other people and learning about their vulnerabilities. Over the years, I've had a wonderful group of singer-performers. In the early group, most of them came from acting and dancing backgrounds. I composed very simple music for them and sang the more complex material with the organ or piano myself. Then, at a certain point in the mid-1970s, I wanted to work with more complex musical textures, so I started working with people who came more from a singing background. I had a wonderful ensemble throughout the '80s. We played all over the place—in clubs, in churches and concerts halls. Then, with the opera *ATLAS*, a new group came in. I'm still working with them to this day. I've always had such wonderful luck. I have tried very hard to choose people not only for their artistry and musicianship but also for their generosity and spirit and the kind of radiance that they have as people. We've always had a wonderful playful spirit of working on this music.

I feel that my work is only a pretext to offering experience of the radiance of these people. I have an idea of a particular piece, and I work very hard to perfect that form but, in fact, that is only an armature; it's really more about these people's energy. I've been lucky enough to work with people from all over the world of different ages and backgrounds. That's been a strong part of my work.

That's probably as much as I want to talk about right now. I'd like to sing a little; then you can ask me questions and I will answer them. The first thing I'd like to sing for you is a piece called *Porch*, which I wrote very early on—I think it was around 1967. It's basically a piece that has a repeated melodic pattern, but is very much about working with different colors and textures in the voice within a simple melodic structure. [Sings].

Now I'd like to do a song from a series called *Light Songs*, which I wrote in the late 1980s. I think of these as duets for solo voice. More than one thing is going on at the same time within one voice. Some of them are like dialogues. In others, more than one layer is going on at the same time. This one is called "Click Song #1." [Sings].

Next I'd like to sing a few songs from the *Songs from the Hill* series. They were all pieces that I wrote sitting up on a hill in New Mexico in the mid-1970s. My sister was living in Placitas, and I would go out to visit her in the summertime. I had been working with keyboard and voice for a few years and hadn't done much a cappella work for a while. My goal was to sit in a particular spot on a hill that I had chosen and compose one song a day. I wrote sixteen of them, or at least started most of them, and then came back to the East Coast and put the ideas into musical forms. I was influenced by the landscape, the magic of New Mexico. I don't feel as if I was imitating what I was hearing, but sitting there, I'm sure that that incredible atmosphere of that place and the desert influenced this music. [Sings].

Now I'd like to sing a few different ones. These are all songs that are inspired by nature and space, but each one also plays with a particular aspect of the voice. This one is called "Wa-lie-oh," consisting of just the syllables that I'm singing. [Sings].

Now I'd like to do three kinds of animal songs from *Songs from the Hill*. The first one is called "Insect," the second one is called "Descending" (it really is another insect piece), and the third is called "Bird Code." I'll sing one more a cappella song, from *Light Songs*. It's called "Click Song #2." [Sings].

I'd like to end this set with a little instrument called a jaw harp, or Jew's harp. I've been playing this pretty much from the late '60s and find it a wonderful instrument for singers. There's a wide range of sound that can be found within it, and so I'd like to share this with you. [Plays and sings].

Thank you very much. Now I would like to continue with some of the pieces that I have written for voice and piano over the years. I'd like to start with one of our earliest song forms and an early piece of mine—a lullaby. Probably this was the first song form because a mother had to find ways to calm her child. Over the years I have worked a lot with the idea that there are archetypal song forms. Within every culture there are lullabies, love songs, marches, laments, and work songs. I like to compose my own manifestations of these song forms that transcend culture. This one is called "Gotham Lullaby." [Sings].

This is also another of my early pieces. It's called "Traveling," and it comes from *Education of the Girlchild.* It's a dance and a journey in 5/4. [Sings].

This next one is actually part of the track of a feature-length film that I made in 1988 called *Book of Days.* I've always been interested in layers of time. Many of my pieces are about time travel. *Book of Days* dealt with the Middle Ages and our time now. It examined the Middle Ages through our eyes, through the filter of the twentieth century. But at the same time, it was looking at our time through the eyes of a young girl from the Middle Ages. She has visions of our time, but she doesn't really know how to explain them to her family and the people who live in her little village. So she's very lonely. It's really a film about a visionary. The one person she can talk to about it is an old madwoman who is actually a seer herself and lives outside the village. The girl tells the madwoman about her apocalyptic visions, like a city that might be burning up and consumed by a plague. There are a lot of parallels between, for example, AIDS and the plague and how certain people were and are blamed for it. Many aspects of human nature seem to stay the same throughout time, and yet each period that we live in is different. The madwoman, after she hears the little girl's vision, answers her with a song about looking at all of time, nature and human nature from an aerial point of view. It sees the folly and beauty of human beings—love, passion, war, violence—from the perspective of nature, the way that nature always renews itself and continues. It's looking at things with a kind of sadness for the world and, at the same time, a kind of compassion and equanimity. This is "Madwoman's Vision." [Sings]. Thank you very much.

QUESTION

Does improvisation play a part in your compositional technique, or even in your performance itself?

MEREDITH MONK

Well, it certainly plays a part in the beginnings of many pieces. My discipline every day is to work vocally or at the piano generating small pieces of material. I find different ways of working with that. It's almost like intuitively coming up with little nodes of music, and then I start seeing how some of these ideas or phrases go together. So, right from the beginning, yes, of course I am working, playing with my voice, working improvisationally to start. Then, little by little, as I start seeing the world of each piece—I think that each piece is a world—I like to dig deeper and deeper into it. Another analogy to some of these forms is a tree with branches, in that the forms—if you listen to some of the *Songs of the Hill*, for example, over the years, you would know that they are the same pieces, but within those forms I have little places where I could branch off if I'm inspired. There are these certain parts of the form where the form branches off. I can play with that material because I always come back to the trunk again.

So, the forms—the beginning, middle, and end—are quite precise. They're very rigorous, yet at the same time there's always room to play. It's the same with the ensemble too; the forms are set, but within them there are some places where we can really play and work with the moment.

QUESTION

I've noticed in your vocal technique there are sounds from all cultures, from all over the world. Did you develop them yourself, just through trying things out, or, in your musical travels, find them and then incorporate them?

MEREDITH MONK

I have always worked with exploring my own voice in my body; that has been my method over the years. I think of the process as developing a vocabulary, built on my own instrument. A lot of people, right from the beginning, started to associate some of what I found with sound that came from other cultures. The way that I try to explain it is that I think that when you work very deeply with your own instrument, there are sounds that transcend culture. If you work with a glottal break, for example, one that has the sound of a yodel (I came upon that as I was playing with my low and upper registers and what it could do, how it could go back and forth), that sound exists in cowboy music, in Swiss yodeling, in some African music, North Carolina hollerin', and many other cultures. So it's really more phylogeny and ontogeny, that just by working with my own instrument with as much honesty as I can, of course within my vocal instrument, I'm going to find different sounds that might make you have associations with other cultures, but the beauty of the human voice is that each of our voices is unique, and at the same time we are part of the world vocal family. I've never been interested in going to a culture, taking something, and using it.

Alvin and I were just talking about that. I was lucky enough to have received a MacArthur grant. They have wonderful meetings and conferences during which you exchange information with other MacArthur fellows. Last week, they had one on animal sounds. They knew I'd be interested in that. There were scientists present (a lot of these MacArthur people are scientists), as well as composer-anthropologist Steven Feld, who has recorded a number of beautiful songs and sounds from Papua New Guinea. Alvin and I were talking about how disgusting it is that sometimes those recordings get into the wrong hands, and then they're totally exploited for commercial gain. That is a cultural imperialist point of view that's not been at all interesting to me over the years.

QUESTION

Do you actually notate your pieces?

MEREDITH MONK

Keyboard works can be notated pretty accurately and some of the things for large choruses are pretty cut-and-dried . . . well, nothing of mine is really cut-and-dried. Actually, it doesn't look very good on the page, the page doesn't really show the principles behind the notes—it's hard to convey that. I believe more in the oral tradition, in a certain way. Like passing it on directly while I'm still alive. But, at the same time, I'm trying to stay very open-hearted to people who want to perform my music. Some of the singers in my ensemble want to perform it, and from time to time there have been other choruses that want to do some of my choral works. So I've been struggling with notating so that other people could be able to sing the music. And I'm still in the midst of this struggle, of how I really feel about this, whether that would be a really good way or not. So, the compromised position is some of the stuff is on paper, but I say that while I'm still alive, I or somebody from my group comes and teaches it to the performers. There have been choruses that don't want anything to do with that; they don't want to bring in a person from outside. In that case I just say no, I'm not interested.

QUESTION

Do you rigorously practice every day?

MEREDITH MONK

Yes, I vocalize every day about forty-five minutes to an hour. When I did the music for Merce Cunningham, I noticed how dancers could go all day long. They take class, and then they do their performance. They're raring to go, whereas most singers that I know, after a certain point, have to rest. You can't sing hour after hour.

My perfect day—if I have a perfect day—is first to do a physical warm up on the floor. Then I vocalize. I take a little break, then compose and work on something. When I go to artists' colonies, I have perfect days. I try to keep my voice exercised every day unless I feel like I need to rest my voice. Then I do.

8

PHILIP GLASS

November 10, 2000

ALVIN LUCIER

It seems like only yesterday that we would be in a downtown loft in New York. Philip Glass and his ensemble would be playing to a small audience. The music was different from anything we had ever heard. It was so loud as to obliterate any sense of being present in a real space. It was repetitive, the same phrase heard over and over, shifting downbeats and accents, abrupt shifts to another succeeding phrase so that there was no sense of time either. We knew the musicians, too. We weren't receiving music from a symphony orchestra that was playing music from someplace else. We weren't being told that what was great and wonderful came from another culture: Brahms, Mozart, and Beethoven. This was music made by our friends, and we didn't know quite what it really meant at that time. We did know that something wonderful was happening.

And it seems like only yesterday that we were sitting up in the balcony of the Brooklyn Academy of Music listening and watching the Philip Glass–Robert Wilson opera, *Einstein on the Beach*. Five and half hours long, repetitious, long images, beautiful music. At the time, we thought to ourselves, "Could this be opera?" If you had asked me if there were a future for opera at that specific moment, I would have said no. Except for a few operas by Berg and Stravinsky and Benjamin Britten, the contemporary scene was barren. Then *Einstein* came along and changed opera forever.

Philip Glass has had an astonishing life as a composer, having made works in every genre—dance, film, opera, world music, solos, and symphonic works, you name it. The Philip Glass Ensemble is still very much in demand, playing his revolutionary repetitive pieces of the 1960s and '70s, such as the three-and-a-half-hour-long *Music in Twelve Parts*. He has achieved a popularity unparalleled by a composer of experimental music.

It's a great thrill for me to introduce Philip Glass.

PHILIP GLASS

We have about an hour. I thought I would speak for about forty minutes and then I'll try to answer a few questions. To talk about music from the angle of theater—that's what Alvin and I decided. We could have talked about a lot of different things. But this is a topic that I happen to know more about than anything, and I think this is a good thing for me too. Theater is something that you really can't learn much about in school. You really learn through living your life in it. And so the kinds of information that I have are things that you might not be able to find so easily.

People have always asked me what kind of music I write—that's always the question: what do you *call* your music. There have been different labels; you know how newspapers and academic people love to have a name for your music. I hated all those names; they were never the names that I called it. But now when people ask me what kind of music I write, I say I write theater music. That answer has the virtue of being absolutely and completely truthful. More than three quarters of my work has been theater work in some way.

When I began as a student, some of my first pieces were theater pieces. I wrote my first one when I was twenty and I started. All the years that I was in music school, I was writing music for dancers and film. When I was twenty-eight, I became a fellow member of the theater company Mabou Mines, and I stayed with them for about twenty years. A lot of the early music that I did was formulated in the context of that company.

In my generation, I was probably the one most committed to working in the theater. And there are a lot of interesting things that happened because of that, a lot of interesting ways of talking about contemporary music and modern music in terms of theater.

Let me go back a little bit and talk about what I actually mean when I say I'm a theater composer. I mean the word in a fairly specific way. For me, theater exists—and I don't just mean theater on a stage; it can be film, it can be dance, it can be various kinds of combinations of film and opera. I look at it this way: I see the four elements that I work with as being text, movement, image, and music. I've been thinking about this for a long time. It's like earth, air, fire, and water. Those are the elements, and everything comes out of some combination of these.

Every one of these fields has an established hierarchy, a kind of structure of how those things get put together. After some time, you begin to figure out what that is. And it becomes very helpful to know what that is, because it makes it easier to work with people, and the expectations are specific for each one. For example, if you are writing music for a play, then the person who will work with you will be the director or the dramaturge. The director will tell you he or she wants music. Maybe you'll write what you want to, but you can't generally put it where you want it to go.

If you're working with a dance company, you have a little more latitude because not many dancers can read music; that saves you a lot of trouble. Almost always, dancers want the music before the dance. Sometimes they'll choreograph the dance before the music, but that's rare. Mostly dancers are still putting steps on beats and they want to know where the beats are. You can do it the other way—it can be done, but it's a little complicated. Even so, the choreographer will actually control how the resources are used. And the main resource in the theater is time.

I remember doing a ballet for Jerry Robbins in the New York City Ballet. He wouldn't let me come to any of the rehearsals until the dress rehearsal. That was how he was. The orchestra sounded terrible. I told him that they couldn't play the music and that we needed a separate music rehearsal. We had only an hour and a half left. He said there was no time for that; he needed to work on the choreography. And that was the end of it. Eventually the orchestra learned the piece. They've done it now for about fifteen years, and by the fifth or sixth year, they played it pretty well. If you go and hear it—it's called *Glass Pieces*—it's good! But the first year, it was just agony; it sounded terrible. But it was Jerry's house—the dance house belonged to the choreographer.

Film is even worse! I'm going to give you all the sad stories; I'll get to the good parts in a minute. With film, there's no question that the film is run by the director. Anyone who's worked in film can tell you endless stories. If you're lucky, you can put the music where you want to, sometimes the director will let you. That's called "spotting" the film. Occasionally the director will let you decide. I was working with Paul Schrader on a film called

Mishima. He was doing it in Japan. I happened to be there doing some concerts, so we got to talking. We spent hours talking about the writer Yukio Mishima and why we were doing a film about him. Finally, I came to the critical crisis and asked Paul where the music should go. He did a wonderful thing. He took the script and threw it across the table and said, "You tell me where it goes." But that almost never happens. I've done about fifteen or sixteen films. It happened one other time with Martin Scorsese. When we were working on *Kundun*, he let me put the music where I thought it should go.

Anyway, the only place in the theater world where the composer is in the composer's house is in the opera house. Perhaps that's why I've written so many operas! I've written about fifteen or sixteen of them. Still, the elements have to be harmonized in some way. I'm still working with a writer, someone with movement, and someone who's creating images. That's on the first level. And then there's another level, including sound, costume, and lighting designers (which is part of the image and part of the sound, but they may not be the actual person that you're working with). That comes into play in the creation of the work.

However, when I decide to write an opera, the first thing I do—and it's important that you do this in the right order, believe me, it'll lead to a lot of trouble—is find the director. If you find the designer before the director, the director will never be happy. You can get away with it a couple times—they'll go along with it—but the director expects to be involved in choosing the designer. So you get the director first, then you get the designer. You may not have a writer. The writer might come in early or later. The work might be based on a story or on a piece of text, so the writer might not be there. When I did *Orfée,* Cocteau was long gone, so I had the scenario of the film. That was a given. But sometimes I've done operas with living writers, so they have to be brought in. This is a very interesting area where the composer actually gets to create the actual working relationship that goes into the piece. And if this is set up carefully, the chances of it working out are much better.

I've gone through collaborations where we've fought like cats and dogs the whole way through. One time the choreographer and I couldn't talk to each other. It was one of the best pieces that we ever did! It doesn't guarantee—it just means that life is a lot more pleasant when you're working where you can talk to everybody. It doesn't guarantee the work is going to be better. It doesn't mean that you'll be happier when you're doing the work. And also, my feeling about collaborations is that I wanted to get the best I could out of every person I was working with. My way of working was to invite them in as cocreators and, very often, if you look at the credits of the operas I've written, I've listed them as coauthors.

The first thing I do is put together a team of people—the writer, the director, the designer, myself. I'll get everyone together and tell him or her that I've got an idea for an opera. When we did the Allen Ginsberg opera, the *Hydrogen Jukebox*, I invited a number of people to be part of that. We spent about a year—that's a luxury, to spend a year working—on the concept.

By the way, that's not all we do. Usually, I'm working on three operas at the same time, but they're all at different stages. One I'm thinking about, one I'm actually writing, and one we're actually building. So I'm involved in different productions all the time, but each production has its own timeline. I find that the first year is very important.

I expect each person to bring his or her best work to the piece. I've found that the best way to let them do their best work is simply to invite them to the project and then let them contribute their own ideas too. I rarely have vetoed something; almost always it's something I didn't think of, and therefore I don't have any idea what they're driving at. I remember working with choreographer Susan Marshall on *Les Enfants Terribles.* It was a combination of dance and opera, based on a film. Since I had initiated the project, it was my project. I asked Susan to do the adaption with me. She would be the choreographer and the director, and we agreed on the costume designs. We did all that together.

The piece had only three characters in it. (Actually, there's a fourth character that comes at the beginning and at the end.) We were talking about the rehearsal period, and she said that she would need eight performers. I reminded her that there were only three performers in the work. She said that she had another idea. And, of course, this meant the whole budget was completely different because we were thinking of travelling with seven or eight people and now it was going to be twelve or thirteen people. That determines how many performances you can have and where you can travel. I had no idea what she was doing. She worked for a couple weeks and invited me to her studio. What she had done was wonderful. Each character—a brother and sister and a friend—was also performed by two dancers. So there were three performers playing each major part.

It was wonderful! What she did sometimes was have the three singers in the front and the others behind. Sometimes they would be on opposite sides of the stage. If one of the actors said something, you could get three different reactions. And I realized that what she had done was most interesting. The kind of things you might hear, and in your head you might have several reactions: I would like to do it; I'm afraid to do it; I can't wait to leave; I don't want to be with you anymore. You might have all those reactions at the same time. Then your computer brain might say that that's a good idea. You figure it out; you do it without even thinking. What Susan did was to portray dramatically everything that went on in the minds of the characters. It was the most wonderful thing. And I had no idea she was going to do that.

So my experience of being with people is that they think of

something that I haven't thought of. That's why I'm doing it to begin with! If I could do the choreography and the design, I wouldn't need any of those people. The fact is that I only know how to do one thing, which is to write the music. I don't know how to write the words, how to do the designs or the movement, so I get involved with all these people. Once I invite them in, they become real partners in the work. That's the dynamic that I try to set up in the way I'm working.

One other thing to talk about is the kind of situation where I have the most freedom. When I say I have control of the environment, I don't actually control all the elements. I'm not interested in controlling all the elements. I discovered very early on that one of the ways that music can—and this is a problem for any composer, any writer, any painter—one of the problems that we have in our work is to create an environment for ourselves in which we're constantly growing and changing. It's the most difficult thing to do. When we're young, we think that the big problem is to find our voice. That is a fairly simple problem. The first problem is to find the voice; the second problem is to get rid of it. And that takes the rest of your life. You never really do it. I've been trying to get rid of my particular way of working since I began, and I've never succeeded.

I've managed to make changes that may seem incremental but over twenty or thirty years have turned out to be big changes. That's about the best you can do. But I've done that through tremendous effort. We learn techniques of working; we become good at certain things. And it becomes very easy for us to repeat what we do. It's as if you were to say that today you are going to walk, talk differently, and write differently. You have to be able to see who you are and what you're trying to do. You have to have an analytic grasp of your style. You may think you are doing something, but you are actually doing something quite different. So there's an analytic perception of your own work that's required.

You very often repeat things that are easy. You see this all the time. There are certain artists I know who have been able to work within one defined area. They go deeper and deeper until their ideas have been resolved in such a high level that you think there was no other way for them to do it.

These choices are based on the personality of the person involved. My particular personality is one to always be looking for new things. When I finished *Einstein on the Beach,* it never occurred to me to write *The Son of Einstein*. Half the people who heard my next opera, *Satyagraha*, were angry and disappointed because it didn't sound like *Einstein*. The other people forgave me. I gave myself permission to do something different. After a while people got used to the fact that I wasn't going to pay any attention to what they said anyway, and they left me alone. That's pretty much the way it is. Now I can do whatever I want because people expect me to do it.

Working in the theater and working with collaborators became almost a guaranteed way for me to do new work: for example, working with Susan Marshall on *Les Enfants Terribles* or Allen Ginsberg on his poetry. When I work with someone I haven't worked with before, they bring something to the table that I didn't anticipate.

Now, let's say that there are always at least four collaborators: a writer, a designer, a director, and a composer. I've often brought in other composers and done collaborative pieces, so that angle can also be changed. I'm doing a piece right now with Australian musicians; that throws a whole other element into the mix. I don't even know what's going to happen, but I will be sure that at least one of three be someone that I haven't worked with before. I almost always include one person I know as my security blanket. It can be a designer I like or it can be the writer. If there's one of the collaborators that I've worked with before, that's enough. The other two, hopefully, will be different. I won't be able to anticipate the dynamic between the working situation and the kind of ideas that are presented. And since I can't anticipate them, I almost always have to do something I hadn't done before. I'll grab on to what I can to make it possible to work at all, and then I'll combine it with some new ideas. So that's how the music begins to change.

I've often said that I don't mind repeating failures, but I will not repeat a success. I'm terrified of that. But the idea of working—with Bob Wilson, we did *Einstein* in 1976. It was a very famous piece and made it possible for the both of us to work in ways that we hadn't before. We didn't work together again until 1984. Then we didn't work again after that until maybe 1991. We spent about eight years apart from each other.

We've developed a very interesting rhythm of working, every eight years we would come together and do a piece. And then I found I would be in touch with Bob's work, and when we began to work together I would love to see, what are the commonalities that were still there? In what ways had he changed? Bob began very much thinking about visual, like paintings. His pieces were big pictures with music. He became more and more involved with movement. Now when he does pieces, he's really a choreographer. So there's been a big shift in his work. So that means that, even as we come to work together, we have a totally intimate working relationship where I know how he works, I know how he thinks. But at the same time, his work has changed.

And the same thing that happened with him has happened with me. When he began working with me, I was working with texts that were in foreign or dead languages, where the main event of the piece would not actually be the singing but would be the instruments. Eventually, I got involved with texts and words, and that led me to work with voices in a different way. Now the main event is the voice, not the instruments. That's a big shift in what I've done.

Now Bob and I have a familiarity with each other. At the same time, there are new things that we bring to the work. In the early pieces, Bob didn't really care about the text. By the time we did *The White Raven* in 1989, we found a writer together. But what we did in *Monsters of Grace*, in 1997—he sent me a text, and I totally disregarded it. I simply picked a different text. I sent it to him and told him that this is the text we were using. It was okay with him. My point was that, as the composer, I had to set the words to the music. And I, for sure, had the primary responsibility for picking the words. On that basis, Bob deferred to me. That's how Bob and I work. There are areas I take for my own. There are those he takes for his own. But we had also had the experience of spending years together so that we knew how each other worked.

There is one thing I wanted to say at the beginning about how we develop—how do we get the training to do this work, and how do you learn to do music theater? With this audience, I think it's worth talking about. It's actually very simple. You spend lots of time in the theater. I decided from the very beginning to go to the rehearsals. For weeks I would sit in the theater with the director. I would watch the lighting designer work, the costumes being fitted. I would talk to the actors and the dramaturge. I wanted to know how many fittings it took to make the costumes, how the lighting worked. I visited the scene shops to see how everything is painted. I wanted to learn every part of the theater from top to bottom.

I also got involved in the producing aspects of it: for example, how much it costs to build a set, how big a truck I needed to move it around. Maybe we could design it differently so the pieces came apart so it could fit into a smaller truck, so the costs were less. All these things became very practical. I often said to people that the theater composer—anyone who works in theater—you end up being the most practical person because you never have enough money, you have to make everything work, everything has to fit in a certain space, into certain time, everything has to fit in a certain budget. If you don't do that, you don't get your piece done.

I was invited to do a piece for the Salzburg Festival, for their millennium, and I went to see the director of the festival. I asked him what I could do. He said that I could do whatever I liked and that this was the biggest festival in Europe. So I said I'd like to have an orchestra and a chorus. He said of course I could have that. Then I asked him if he had a children's choir. He said yes, he did. Then I asked for four soloists. He said I could have five! I never would have been able to do such a large work unless someone had said that I could do whatever I liked. This was my *Symphony Number 5*.

It happened one other time. When I did *The Voyage* at the Met in 1992, I was talking to the designer, Bob Israel, with whom I had worked before. He was designing this amazing piece with spaceships flying around, appearing and disappearing. For the first eight minutes everyone's flying in air! At one point I asked him what the budget was. And he answered that we didn't have a budget. I almost fainted. That's unheard of.

I was just in Boston—I'm talking about doing a piece with two singers. Well, that's another thing you should know, another thing that's very important to understand about theater. Not only do you learn it from being in the theater, but you also begin to understand that there's a tremendous flexibility into how big and how small pieces can be. I've done pieces where there are three singers. I'm doing a ninety-minute, continuously sung opera right now based on Kafka's *In the Penal Colony*. It is scored for two singers and string quintet. It can be done in small theater. I discovered that a theater company might mount a small opera if they can fit it into their normal budget. It was performed six or eight times in Seattle. They have put it away, and maybe they'll schedule it again next year. They're doing it right now in Chicago, for eight performances a week for five weeks. These theaters are about as big as this room. We're talking about two or three hundred people at most, more often 180, 190. In June, it will be done in a little theater in New York. They'll do forty performances, too. So here's an opera that's being performed 120 times in one year, which is completely astonishing. By the way, it's not a good idea to call these works chamber operas because people tend not to want to perform them. I simply call them pocket operas.

In music theaters these days, the director often assumes a kind of authorship role where he or she puts together all the components. Peter Sellars, JoAnne Akalaitis, Peter Brook, and Bob Wilson do that. Meredith Monk of course does everything; writes, dances, choreographs, and composes the music. Most people are good at just one thing; then they organize everything around them. But as a composer—I'm talking to the composers here—the more you know about the mechanics of theater, the more flexibility you'll have in what you can do. You'll work more. My old pieces are still being done as I'm working on new ones. The question is, who can I get to build this piece? I spend a fair amount of time talking people into doing productions. It's not that easy; everything costs money. People are interested, but actually getting them to make a budget is a problem. Budgets can go from $100,000 to $100,000,000. Sometime you may get away [with] as little as $40,000 or $50,000. But then you're really getting down to *really* small budgets. Once you start paying people, money will disappear very quickly.

Another way to do it is what I did with the theater company that I started with, Mabou Mines. I was the composer, and there were two directors and three actors. Basically we built everything ourselves. We did that for years until we got other people to start building.

Well, I think that you can always do a piece. I think that everything's expensive and no one wants to do it, but you can still do it. Things aren't very different now than they were thirty years ago. In fact, they're somewhat worse. We're at a time now where the theater, opera, and film world has become oriented toward the idea of entertainment. Even opera companies want to do works that are entertainment pieces. Now, of course, opera is a place where entertainment and art always came together; that was the great power of the medium. You had something like *Rigoletto,* which was fun to watch. It was a fabulous piece of music. *The Magic Flute* was hugely popular.

There's been a big shift more toward entertainment and head counting. In a way, it was easier when we had little places like La MaMa on East 4th Street in New York City. Ellen Stewart didn't care if anybody came. Now almost no one has that attitude. Everyone wants to know how many people are coming. Theater companies have boards of directors who want to know . . . it's a nightmare.

However, you can still do it! There's still always some jackass that will let you into his place and let you do a piece. You can always find someplace to do your work. In some ways it's more difficult, in some ways it's easier. When I did *Einstein on the Beach*, I didn't know anyone writing an opera but myself, and now I don't know anyone who isn't writing an opera. Alvin, are you writing an opera?

ALVIN LUCIER
What?

PHILIP GLASS
Yes, are you writing an opera?

ALVIN LUCIER
I'm not writing an opera.

PHILIP GLASS

He's the only one!

ALVIN LUCIER

But if you gave me a good idea . . .

PHILIP GLASS

But he would! We've got about fifteen minutes, let's do a few questions. I think I covered, quickly and roughly, how I'm working.

QUESTION

I had a question dealing with situations where, having to intertwine several disciplines, you seem to be talking about it in terms of different trajectories that come together, and you come to some kind of functional understanding. Then you go off, you continue on your way, maybe you meet up with someone for a second time. I know that you have collaborated with Richard Serra, and, in addition to the people you mentioned, the question would be, have you ever found working with these people—their work and their conceptual status—so powerful that it's affected your work in a way that was not ephemeral?

PHILIP GLASS

There are two answers for that. You get together in the first year. In the second year, you go off and do your own work; in the third year, you put it back together. That's roughly the way it works.

There is a moment when the composer sits down and writes the music. There's a moment when the designer is alone. I try to make everyone do their work first, so I have all the texts and designs. Theater people have that kind of flexibility. I was working with Doris Lessing on an opera recently, and when I was setting the libretto to music, I called her every day to talk about changes in the texts that had to be made for reasons of singing. That went on for months. She was in London and I was in Nova Scotia, but we were in touch all the time.

When we were doing *Orphée* we had to create an underworld and the ordinary world at the same time, and the director had to see how that was going to work. We couldn't even start conceptualizing or building anything until we had solved problems of that kind. We worked separately but were never out of touch. No one goes to Mars and the other to the moon, and then they get together. You can't really work like that.

Working with other people has completely changed what I've done. It's happened most in collaborations with musicians more than with sculptors or painters. The times I've worked with other musicians have been very striking. For example, I remember working with Foday Suso, a *griot* (storyteller) from the Gambia. We were composing music to go with *Les Paravents* (*The Screens*) by Genet. I knew Foday and his music, but I had no idea how we were going to work together. The first day, the director, JoAnne Akalaitis, she said, "We're going to start with the first thing, and I'm going to need music *here*." I knew right away that, working with Foday, I wouldn't really be writing music. He would play his music, and I would play along with him, and we would arrive at something through playing together. We could notate it later.

Foday said that he would have to tune his instrument, a seventeen-stringed harp-like kora. He played a note—it was kind of like a D. Then he played the next note up the scale, and I asked him what he called that note. He said simply that that was the next note. Then he played another note. I asked him what he called that one. He replied that it was simply the note after that. It suddenly occurred to me that he didn't have names for the notes. It was almost as if the ground disappeared beneath my feet.

As a young musician, I remember my very first flute lesson. I was maybe seven or eight years old. My teacher handed me the flute and showed me how to hold it. Then he showed me a note on the page. It was a B-natural. He told me to blow. Then he put it all together: the instrument, the note, the name of the note, the way it looked on the page, and the sound. That was my first lesson. And all my lessons were like that. So, for me, notes always had names. Suddenly I was in a world where they didn't. I almost fainted. I was so shocked I didn't know how to proceed.

The same thing—not so catastrophic—happened with Ravi Shankar, when I worked with him years before that. We were doing a piece together, and I was trying to notate something he was playing. We were doing this clapping thing. You've probably all done some of that, working with Indian rhythm, tala, and learning to do it by speaking it, but not writing it. And I wasn't getting what he was saying, so he said, "Here Phil, hold the pencil—you'll think better." He was right! As I held the pencil, I could figure out what he was saying!

In situations with composers like that, I've been completely thrown into areas that changed the way I thought about music. I know that there's a well-developed world music program here. I got involved with world music in the 1960s in India and Africa. I never had formal training; I simply worked with musicians.

I remember working with Ravi Shankar in 1965. Some other musicians there were playing some music, and I was trying to write it down. Alla Rakha kept saying that it was not right. I was still using bar lines. I had no idea how the music worked. But a couple hours later, I simply erased all the bar lines, and within two or three hours, I was notating their music in a way that the accents were in the right places. That was the day that Ravi threw me into the deep end of the pool. I swam to the top! It was a profoundly traumatic experience.

QUESTION

I'm interested to know how actors and singers fit into these collaborations, or do they?

PHILIP GLASS

I have the most contact with singers. When possible, I'll write for a singer I know, although I'm not always able to do that. Sometimes I will audition singers, so even if I don't know them personally, I've at least heard them.

I was already forty before I began learning how to write for the voice. I would ask each singer how her vocal part worked. Very quickly, singers will tell you things such as where the break in their voice is, that they can go up here but have to go down there. So by the mid-80s, I was writing very well for the voice. Several singers told me to look at Handel, how he moves the voice through the low, middle, and the high parts of their ranges. A singer can sing Handel for a long time and never get tired.

I began holding auditions, sometimes fifty-five singers in one afternoon. I would ask the singers [to sing] certain pieces of Handel's or mine. Very rarely would I let them sing Verdi, whose vocal parts are often in the top of their range and accompanied by a large orchestra. If a singer has a big operatic voice, it's not going to help me very much if I'm going to be in a little concert hall with four musicians. I often think of the voice in terms of where the singer is going to be singing.

It is not the same with actors. There's usually a song in a Shakespeare play. And for sure, the director will ask one of the actresses to sing. And for sure, they can't. The last time I did a Shakespeare play, I asked the director to let me audition the actors before she decided who's going to sing the song. Then I could tell her who could and who couldn't sing. I told her which ones could sing. And she picked one of the ones who couldn't sing. I asked her why, after we had gone through all that, did she pick that particular actress. She won't be able to sing what I write. She said that I may not have noticed, but the actress she chose only had one leg. She wanted to work with someone who had a prosthetic leg. She had to walk in a certain way, and the director wanted to make that part of the piece.

In the opera house it's not quite like that. Recently I wrote a piece for Herb Perry, a bass baritone. We needed a cover for him, so we asked his identical twin brother, Eugene, also a baritone. However, the best notes for Eugene were a whole step higher than for Herb. I ended up having to transpose five of the scenes for Eugene. So when he sang, five of the scenes were in a different key. I hope the librarian gets it right when they put out the music.

QUESTION

Could you talk a little bit about the piece that you did at the ABT [American Ballet Theatre]?

PHILIP GLASS

What was the piece?

QUESTION

I don't remember what it was called.

PHILIP GLASS

Well, what I can tell you is that sometimes people will choose five or six of my pieces and make a ballet out of them. That happens a lot. Often I don't have very much to do with it. The best situation is when a choreographer and I collaborate on a piece. That has happened quite a few times, particularly with Lucinda Childs, Twyla Tharp, and Jerry Robbins. Strange things can still happen because the worlds of dance and music are so different. I remember going out on tour once with a dance company. I took class with them for the whole tour because I wanted to know what it was like for the body to move in that way. The dancers laughed at me, but they were happy to have me there. I took class every afternoon. I couldn't do the combinations. I fell down a couple of times, but I wanted to be involved in the dance in some way, and this was one way of doing it. It was a lot of fun to work with dancers, but also frustrating at times because we look at the work in very different ways.

One little story: I was making a piece with Twyla Tharp. When I sent her the tape, she said that the piece was completely different. I listened to the tape, and it sounded the same to me. I asked her to tell me what was different. She said that it was twice as long between the first and second movement. She meant the space in between the two movements. It wasn't hard to make the spaces identical. I had no idea that she was listening to the silences, and I was listening to the music. She was dancing through the silences. Well, anyway . . .

ALVIN LUCIER

Thank you very much, Phil.

About the Editor

ALVIN LUCIER is an American composer of experimental music and sound installations. He is the author of *Music 109: Notes on Experimental Music* and coauthor, with Douglas Simon, of *Chambers.* Lucier was awarded the Lifetime Achievement Award by the Society for Electro-Acoustic Music and received an honorary Doctorate of Arts from the University of Plymouth, England. He taught at Brandeis University and Wesleyan University, and retired from the latter in 2011.

About the Composers

MARYANNE AMACHER was born on February 25, 1939, in Kane, Pennsylvania. She studied with the composer George Rochberg at the University of Pennsylvania, and later privately with the German avant-garde composer Karlheinz Stockhausen. Amacher was known for large-scale, site-specific sound installations that explore the propagation of sound in architectural spaces. Her work often focused on psychoacoustic phenomena in which sound is generated from within the ear. Amacher collaborated extensively with John Cage and the Merce Cunningham Dance Company. In 1998 she received a *Foundation for Contemporary Arts Grants to Artists Award* as well as the *Prix Ars Electronica Award* in the "digital arts" category. In the last decade of her life, Maryanne Amacher taught electronic music at Bard College. She died on October 22, 2009, in Rhinebeck, New York.

ROBERT ASHLEY was born on March 28, 1930, in Ann Arbor, Michigan. He was educated at the University of Michigan and the Manhattan School of Music, following which he returned to the study of psychoacoustics and speech patterns at the University of Michigan Speech Research Laboratory.

He rose to prominence in the 1960s as a founder and organizer of the ONCE Group and was a member of the Sonic Arts Union, a collective of experimental composers that included David Behrman, Gordon Mumma, and Alvin Lucier. Throughout his life Ashley was fascinated by the musical nature of speech. *Perfect Lives*, the first of over thirty operas for television, was premiered on British television in 1984 and has since been broadcast throughout the world. His final opera, *Crash*, premiered after his death at the 2014 Whitney Biennial. Ashley died in New York that same year.

PHILIP GLASS was born on January 31, 1937, in Baltimore, Maryland. He studied at the Peabody Institute in Baltimore, the University of Chicago, and the Julliard School before moving to Paris to study with the legendary pedagogue Nadia Boulanger. There he met Ravi Shankar, from whom he developed an interest in Indian classical music. Much of his music, particularly the early works, is characterized by his use of the incessant repetition of rhythmic and melodic patterns creating mesmerizing and trance-like compositions. In 1968, he founded the Philip Glass Ensemble, a group with which he continues to perform. His opera *Einstein on the Beach,* on which he collaborated with Robert Wilson, earned him international acclaim in 1976 and continues to be performed today at venues around the world. Philip Glass is one of the most prolific composers in the world today, having produced eleven symphonies, eighteen operas, thirty-eight film scores, and seven string quartets, as well as numerous solo pieces and works for theater and dance. Philip Glass has collaborated with a wide range of artists, including Alan Ginsburg, Jerome Robbins, Twyla Tharp, David Bowie, and Martin Scorsese, and has been awarded three Academy Award Nominations.

MEREDITH MONK, born November 20, 1942, is a composer, theater director, vocalist, filmmaker, choreographer, and early pioneer of performance art. Her vocalizations are legendary, incorporating a wide variety of extended techniques that reach beyond language. After graduating from Sarah Lawrence in 1964, Monk went on to win many awards, including a MacArthur "Genius" Grant and two Guggenheim fellowships. In 1968, Monk founded the House, a company dedicated to exploring concepts of interdisciplinary performance. In 1978 she formed the Meredith Monk & Vocal Ensemble and recorded several highly successful albums, including her first widely celebrated *Songs from the Hill/Tablet* in 1979. *Atlas, an Opera in Three Parts*, was premiered by the Houston Grand Opera in February 1991. Meredith Monk continues to compose numerous works for orchestra, chamber ensembles, and solo instruments, with commissions from Carnegie Hall, Michael Tilson Thomas and the San Francisco Symphony, the Kronos Quartet, and the Los Angeles Master Chorale, among others.

STEVE REICH was born on October 3, 1936, in New York City. He graduated with honors in philosophy from Cornell in 1957. For the next two years he studied composition with Hal Overton, and from 1958 to 1961, he studied with William Bergsma and Vincent Persichetti at the Julliard School of Music. He received an MA in music from Mills College in 1963, where he studied with Luciano Berio and Darius Milhaud. Reich's discovery and use of phasing and other innovative techniques has helped him earn a place as one of the greatest living composers. He has had a significant impact on contemporary music, influencing artists from Brian Eno to Radiohead. He was awarded the 2009 Pulitzer Prize in Music for his composition *Double Sextet*. The same year he received multiple Grammy awards for his *Music for 18 Musicians* and *Different Trains*. Steve Reich was awarded the Gold Medal in Music by the American Academy of Arts and Letters and has received honorary doctorates from the Royal College of Music in London, the Juilliard School, the Liszt Academy in Budapest, and the New England Conservatory of Music.

JAMES TENNEY was born on August 10, 1934, in Silver City, New Mexico. He was a highly regarded pianist, composer, and music theorist. A pioneer in computer music as well as an important character in the Fluxus artist movement, Tenney is known for his conceptually driven and computer-aided compositions. He studied composition under many influential composers, including Edgard Varèse and John Cage. He was the cofounder and conductor of the Tone Roads Chamber Ensemble and has performed alongside Steve Reich, Philip Glass, and John Cage. He taught at the Polytechnic Institute of Brooklyn, the California Institute for the

Arts, the University of California, and York University. James Tenney died on August 24, 2006, in Valencia, California.

CHRISTIAN WOLFF was born on March 8, 1934, in Nice, France. He moved with his family to the United States in 1941, where he studied piano with Grete Sultan and composition with John Cage. The youngest member of the New York School of composers, which included Earle Brown, John Cage, and Morton Feldman, Wolff continues to write numerous works for unlikely combinations of disparate or indeterminate instrumentation, many of which use political texts. He studied classics at Harvard University and later went on to become the Strauss Professor of Music and Classics at Dartmouth College. Wolff's honors and awards include honorary degrees from the California Institute of the Arts and Huddersfield University in the United Kingdom, as well as a DAAD Berlin fellowship and a lifetime achievement award from the state of Vermont.

LA MONTE YOUNG was born in a log cabin in Bern, Idaho, on October 14, 1935. He attended Los Angeles City College and, in 1958, received a BA from UCLA. From 1958 to 1960 he did graduate work at Berkeley with composer Seymour Shifrin, at which time he composed *Trio for Strings*, a work whose use of extremely long tones was the precursor to the subsequent development of the minimalist aesthetic and drone music. In the summer of 1959 he traveled to Darmstadt, where he met David Tudor, who introduced him to the music and writings of John Cage. He moved to New York City in 1960 to study electronic music with Richard Maxfield at the New School for Social Research. In 1970 he developed an interest in North Indian classical music and began studying under the Hindustani vocal master Pandit Pran Nath. His five-and-a-half-hour work *The Well-Tuned Piano,* which Young himself regards as his masterpiece, is the definitive example of the use of just intonation in experimental music. In 2002, Young, along with Marian Zazeela and Jung Hee Choi, founded the Just Alap Raga Ensemble, a Hindustani classical music ensemble based in New York City.